Draw in 4! Over 100 4-Step Sketches to Boost Your Drawing Confidence

Ben Crothers

Published by Ben Crothers, 2019.

DRAW IN 4! OVER 100 4-STEP SKETCHES TO BOOST YOUR DRAWING CONFIDENCE

First edition. March 4, 2019.

ISBN: 978-1393507925

Written by Ben Crothers.

Draw in 4 is dedicated to the thriving global community of sketchers, sketchnoters, doodlers, urban sketchers, graphic recorders and graphic facilitators. We draw for fun, we draw for good, and we draw for change!

Draw in 4!

Over 100 4-Step Sketches

to Boost Your Drawing Confidence

By

Ben Crothers

Thank you

I really love the way this book has come about.

One of the drawing techniques I included in my book *Presto Sketching: The Magic of Simple Drawing for Brilliant Product Thinking and Design*[1] is the **foundation lines technique**, a universal technique that's a real winner for increasing confidence and capability in sketching. Once *Presto Sketching*[2] was published), I started putting up simple four-step practice sketches on Instagram[3] as a way to show the foundation lines technique in action.

Since then, there have been more than 120 sketches, with tons of hearts and comments, and quite a few people posting *their* sketches using the four-step sketches, too. I'm really grateful to the Instagram community for their encouragement, and this has spurred me on to not only keep doing the sketches themselves, but to bundle up most of the existing ones into this book.

Thanks also to several guiding lights in the visual thinking/ communication domain who have been a huge source of encouragement and wisdom to me as I've been doing these 4-step sketches: Brandy Agerbeck, Sunni Brown, Dave Gray, Eva-Lotta Lamm, Matthew Magain, Mike Rohde, and Jessie Shternshus. Your generosity of time and friendship means a lot!

Thanks and hugs to Linette Voller and Ingrid Nouwens for casting their eagle eyes over the draft of this book.

Massive thanks and hugs go to my family, not only for their support and encouragement, but also for giving me lots of ideas along the way.

---

1. *http://prestosketching.com/*

2. *http://prestosketching.com/*

3. https://www.instagram.com/prestosketching/

3

And I thank *you* for backing yourself enough to read this book, and for wanting to get better and better at sketching and visual communication. I really hope that doing these practice sketches helps you to amp up your capability and confidence!

About this book

This is your visual phrase book

The more I teach about visual expression in general and sketching in particular, the more I see that people *want* more visual expression in their lives, but need more ways to help them to *learn* it and *apply* it.

Visual expression is a language, and just like any other language, it contains the equivalent of letters, words, sentences, and so on. Simple strokes ('letters') can be combined into shapes ('words'), which can then be combined to form simple pictures ('phrases').

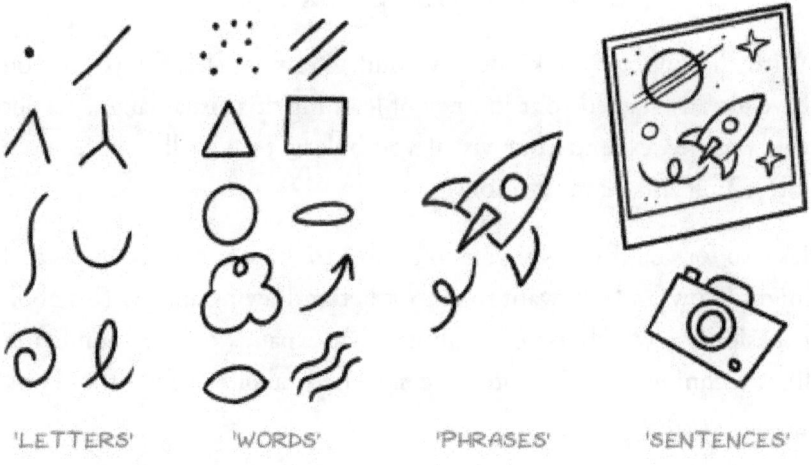

'LETTERS'   'WORDS'   'PHRASES'   'SENTENCES'

The pictures you draw can become more complex, layered and nuanced ('sentences'). If you think about sketching in this way, you can sketch just about anything you want by breaking it down into these components.

And just like written and spoken languages, it has different *ways to use it*, such as sketchnoting for *visual* learning, storyboards for *visual* communication of ideas and entertainment, infographics for *visual* explanation, scribing for *visual* conversations... the list is endless!

Imagine you've landed in a country where you don't know the local language. You probably don't want to start by learning all the complexities of their grammar. But you probably *do* want to know how to say things like "Can I have two beers please?" and "Where is the beach?" In short: you want a phrase book.

Draw in 4! is your visual phrase book. It won't teach you everything, far from it! But it *will* increase the number and variety of words you can 'speak' in this wonderful language.

Who is this book for?

With that 'phrase book' idea in mind, **Draw in 4!** is for you if you have already started your journey of learning this visual language, but you want to expand your visual vocabulary, to – well – have more interesting visual conversations.

It's also for you if you struggle to be able to draw as well as others you might know, and you want to unlock better drawing ability. This book is basically a workbook of examples that expands on the foundation lines technique that I wrote (and sketched) about in my other book *Presto Sketching*[1].

I'll get into the foundation lines technique a bit later, but I'll say up front: it's a great way to increase your powers of observation, and translating what you see (either physically or in your mind's eye) into your drawing.

Draw in 4! is also for you if you are a:

---

1. *http://prestosketching.com/*

- **Sketchnoter, scribe or graphic recorder** – increase the speed, quality and efficiency of the objects and visual metaphors you need to draw
- **Teacher** – a trove of drawing activities for students
- **Parent** – lots of fun things to draw with your kids
- **Designer, illustrator or art student** – a workbook of examples to practice, to increase your skills of observation and synthesis

Oh, and of course this book is for you if you just love drawing like I do, and you're always on the lookout for more ways to enjoy drawing!

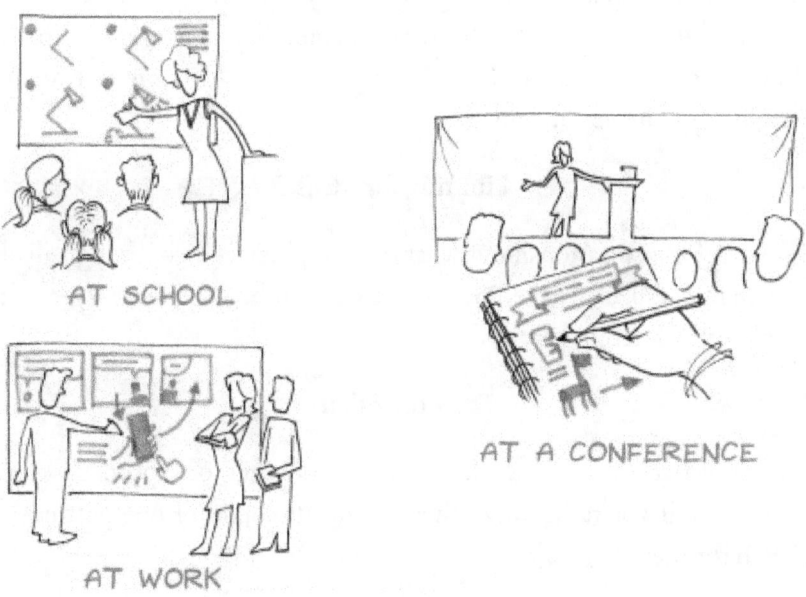

AT SCHOOL

AT A CONFERENCE

AT WORK

How to use this book

Draw in 4! is a workbook of sketching practice examples. It's here to help you practice. Thinking of the foreign language analogy I used earlier, you won't be fluent straight away; new words and phrases need to be practiced over and over, before you can speak confidently and fluently. With that in mind, there are different ways you can use this book:

Starting out

All of the practice sketches are grouped into sections by theme, and each section has sketches *generally* in order of difficulty. So, if you're just starting out and want to focus on the easier ones, just dip into the beginning of each section, and practice the easiest sketches first.

Wanting a laser-focused workout

Do you have something coming up where you know you'll be drawing lots of things to do with the same theme? Say you're going to be drawing lots of hands; go through the *Hands and handling* section, to develop your muscle memory.

Hunting for ideas

Looking for inspiration about what to draw? Have a flick through all of the themes, especially the Pop culture and symbols section, to get you thinking in different ways.

Teaching others

Each practice sketch is made to fit on one page or laptop/desktop screen. So, if you're helping others, print off copies of one particular sketch for them to try.

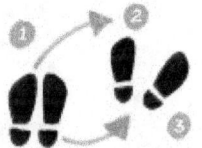

STARTING OUT

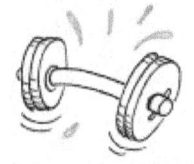

SKETCHING WORKOUT

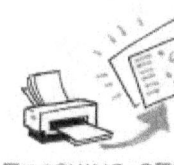

HUNTING FOR IDEAS

TEACHING OTHERS

Getting started

If **Draw in 4!** is your visual phrasebook, then you'll need something to write you phrases with, and a handy sketchbook (or something similar), to keep with you day by day.

A bit of practice goes a long way, so get ready to treat each of these practice sketches as exactly that: a way to repeat each object with foundation lines until you don't need the foundation lines at all.

Materials

When it comes to the question of what materials to use when sketching, *normally* I say, "Anything and everything!". I know from my own experience (and others' experience) that great ideas don't wait until you have *just* the right marker, *just* the right paper, *just* the right time of day, wearing *just* the right socks, and so on.

I *also* know, though, that different people have different attitudes toward what materials to use, and it's important to understand what works best for *you*.

But, for **Draw in 4!** I'm going to be a bit more prescriptive. These practice sketches use a specific technique called 'foundation lines', which needs two basic types of mark-making tools:

- **Foundation lines** – Use something light and/or lightly-coloured, like a pencil, or coloured markers
- **Final lines** – Use a black marker

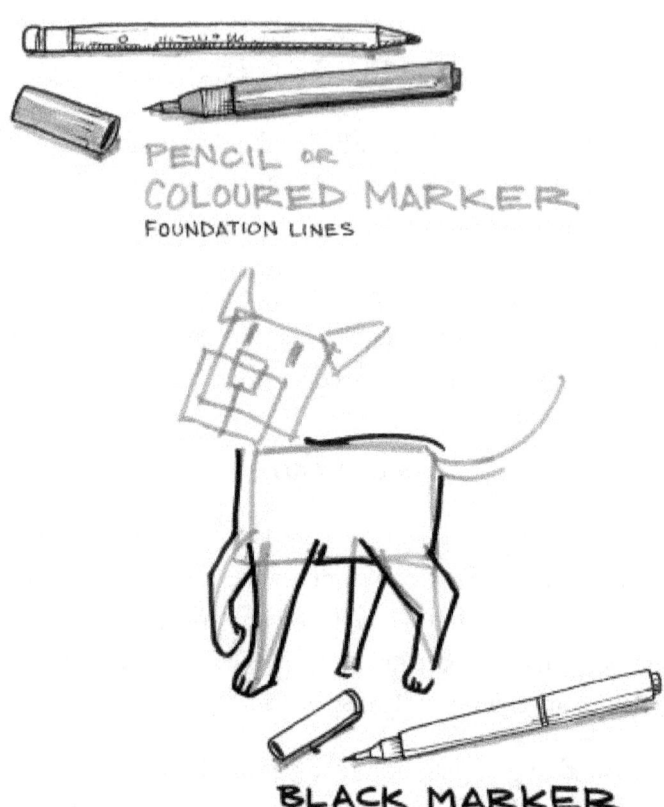

PENCIL or
COLOURED MARKER
FOUNDATION LINES

BLACK MARKER
FINAL LINES

With those two constraints in mind, go nuts with trying different *types* of colour, line thickness, and so on.

I've used different colours and types of markers throughout the examples in this book on purpose, to illustrate this.

The foundation lines technique

All of the practice sketches in this book use foundation lines to help you tackle each sketch. Foundation lines is a universal drawing technique that many art schools teach, and many artists and illustrators practice, across every domain from technical drawing to abstract art.

As you can see from the picture here, foundation lines help you to put on 'X-ray goggles' and look at any object 'inside out' rather than only the outside of the object. They make observing and drawing much easier by helping you to mentally separate a complex object into a set of simple shapes.

The process goes a bit like this:

1. **Look.** Really look at what it is you're sketching.
2. **See the shapes.** Look 'into' the object and break it into several simple shapes.
3. **Sketch the shapes.** Draw those rough basic geometric shapes in light colour.
4. **Sketch over the top.** Sketch the object in black using the foundation lines as a guide.

This technique is a really forgiving way of sketching something. Rather than having to rely on an eraser all the time, you can 'find the right line' by sketching several foundation lines instead, until you get a line that is 'right enough'.

Just doing this and experiencing the freedom from the eraser is a great step forward alone!

1 TAKE A REALLY GOOD LOOK AT WHAT IT IS YOU'RE GOING TO DRAW...

2 LOOK 'INTO' IT, AND MENTALLY BREAK IT INTO SIMPLE SHAPES...

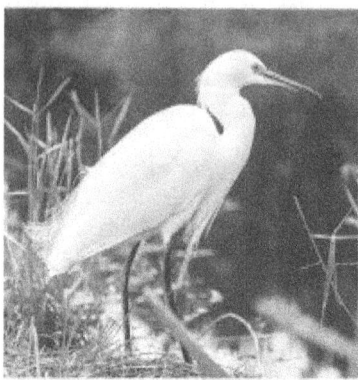

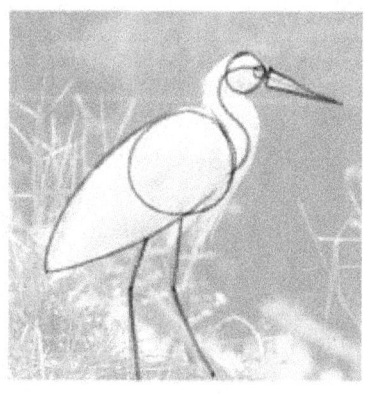

3 SKETCH THE SHAPES THAT YOU SEE AS LIGHT FOUNDATION LINES

4 SKETCH OVER THE TOP IN BLACK, USING THOSE FIRST LINES AS A GUIDE.

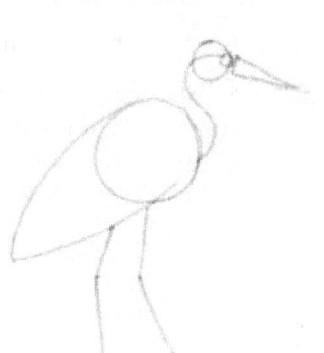

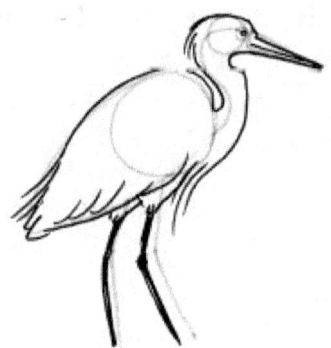

Foundation lines are training wheels

Treat this foundation lines technique like training wheels on a bike. Of course, you can learn to ride a bike *without* training wheels, but it might take a little longer, and your confidence might take a hit while you get up to speed.

The same applies to drawing: you can learn to draw in all sorts of ways, and never go *near* any foundation lines, but your confidence might take a hit in the meantime.

You can use this foundation lines technique as a way to get used to observing whatever it is you're drawing, and getting a mental handle on how to actually draw it. Once you've drawn something a few times with foundation lines, you'll find that it'll 'imprint' itself in your brain, like a blueprint that you file away in your 'things I can draw confidently' filing cabinet. By the time you practise it a few times, you build up the muscle memory for drawing that thing, and then you won't need foundation lines anymore.

You'll start to notice that you can 'see' the foundation lines with your mind's eye already there on the page, or whiteboard, or whatever it is you're drawing on, and you'll be able to draw it confidently in one go.

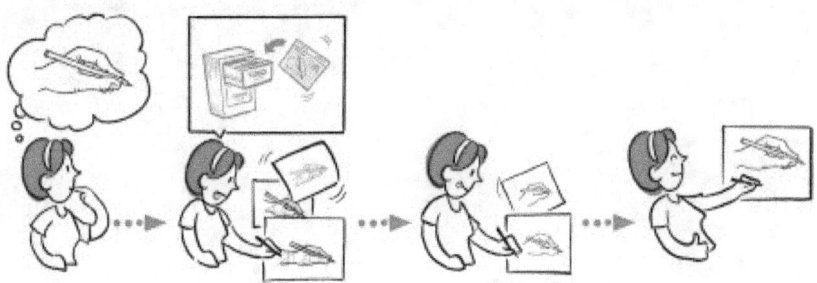

That's what we're aiming for here. Confident, capable, off-the-cuff drawing. So with that goal in mind, let's get sketching, shall we?

House and home

There are lots of common household objects around you at home that make perfect sketching subjects, especially if you want to do some practice to up your sketching game. Like all of these sections, the easiest objects are first, and get gradually trickier throughout the section.

As you sketch these objects, take a look around your own home, to find other objects to try sketching as well.

What you'll draw in this section

Book, wrench, cactus, scales, toilet, desk lamp, bird cage, lava lamp, drill, camera, blender, bed, couches, medicine bottle, and a chair.

Book

Let's start with a reasonably easy one: an open book. Start by doing the foundation lines with a coloured marker, and then finish the drawing with a black marker over the top.

Notice the thicker line for the cover around the outside, too. A little bit of neatness and care goes a long way here!

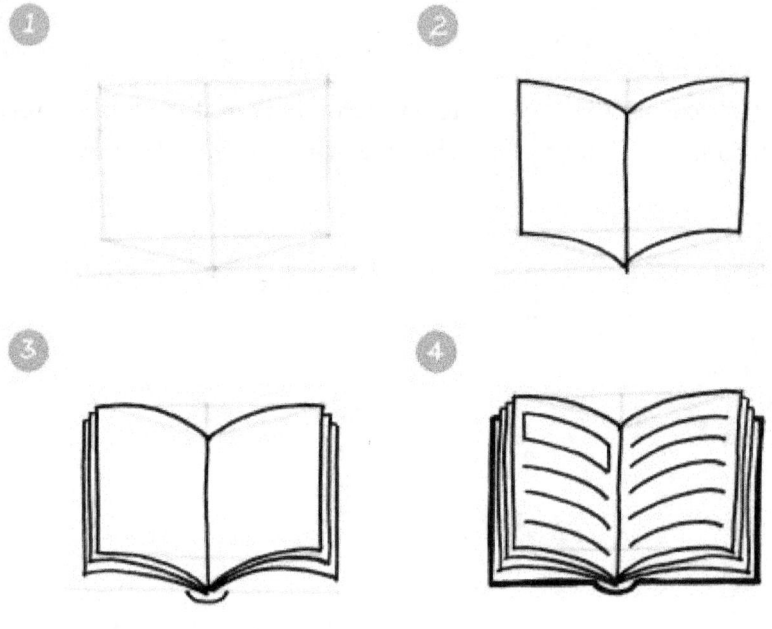

Wrench

Spanners and wrenches come in handy when you need a sketch to represent 'fixing something', or 'tools' or maybe 'support'. But when you *really* need to fix something, you need this adjustable spanner (or wrench).

Use the foundation lines of a circle and two diagonal lines to 'locate' the jaws of your adjustable wrench and the handle. Finishing it off with the little screw-thread that moves the jaws is a nice touch, too.

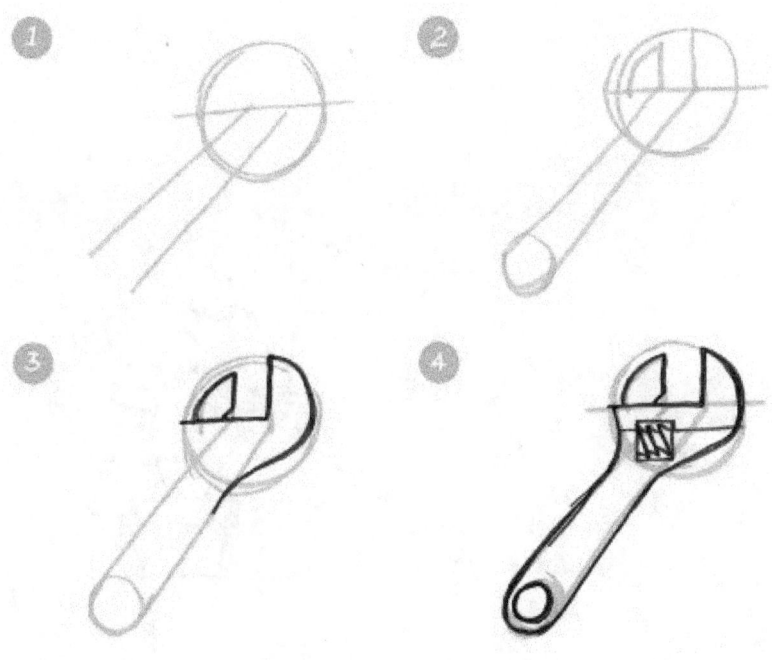

Cactus

Cacti are super fun to draw. You can draw just about any bunch of blobs, go around the outside with a dark line, and it'll look like a cactus! Start this one with one large oval, plus a bit of a rhomboid shape to show where the pot will go (1). Add in a few more ovals wherever you like, with each oval getting smaller (3). Fun, hey? Try doing variations of your cactus using longer ovals, or even rectangles or sausage shapes.

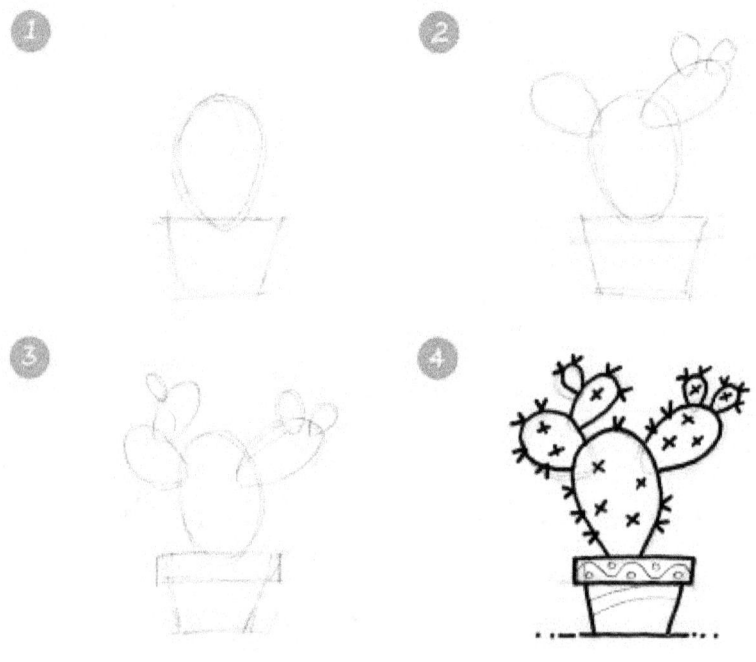

Scales

More and more kitchens these days have digital weighing scales that come with accompanying apps, that do all sorts of things, like track your weighing patterns, share what you're weighing on social media, and talk with your fridge and local supermarket about what food you're weighing. Actually, I just made all that up. The point is, a good ol' analogue weighing scales set is not only a dependable asset in the kitchen, it's also fun to draw.

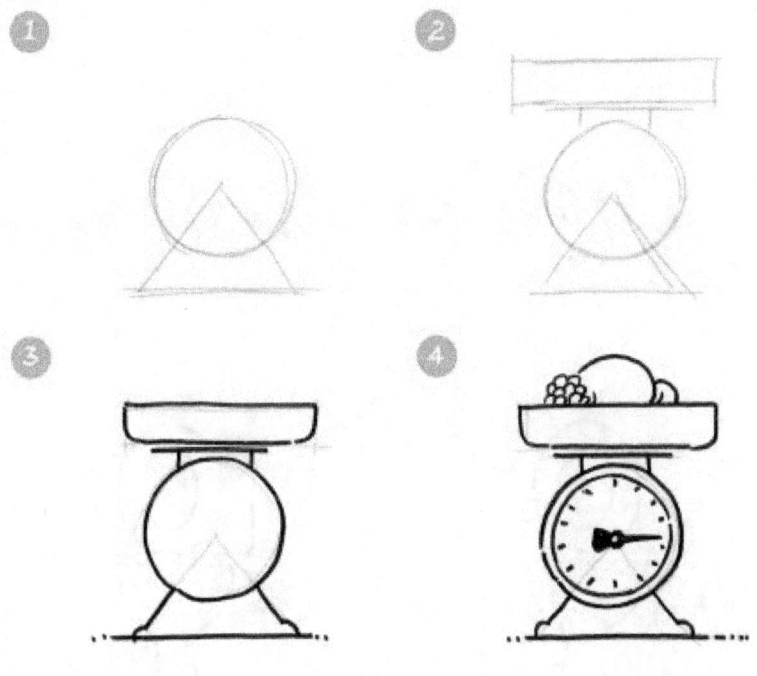

Toilet

You might have heard that the toilet was invented by Sir Thomas Crapper. Sir Crapper (1836-1910) was certainly a plumber, and he improved the toilet (as we know it), but he didn't invent it. That particular honour goes to Sir John Harington, a 16th-century courtier of Queen Elizabeth I.

That's something interesting to ponder, as you sketch this remarkable piece of technology, isn't it? Go ahead and accessorise your toilet if you want to.

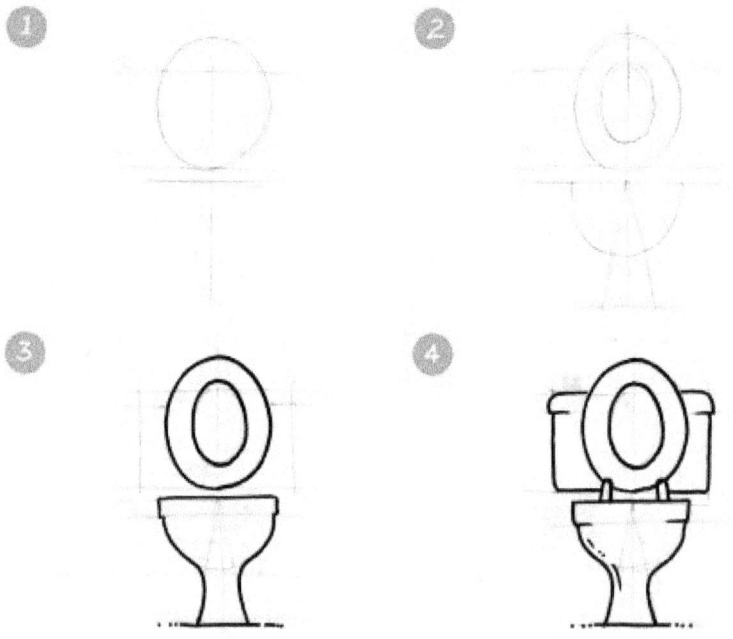

Desk lamp

Desk lamps come in many shapes and sizes, but this one is a pretty popular sort of desk lamp.

Use your foundation lines to sketch the armature and base (1), followed by a triangle and oval for the 'head' of the lamp (2). Make sure your final lines on the armature are nice and straight, and you'll end up with a much more satisfying result (3). All that's left is to 'switch on' (sorry) a bit of detail on the head of the lamp, and you're done!

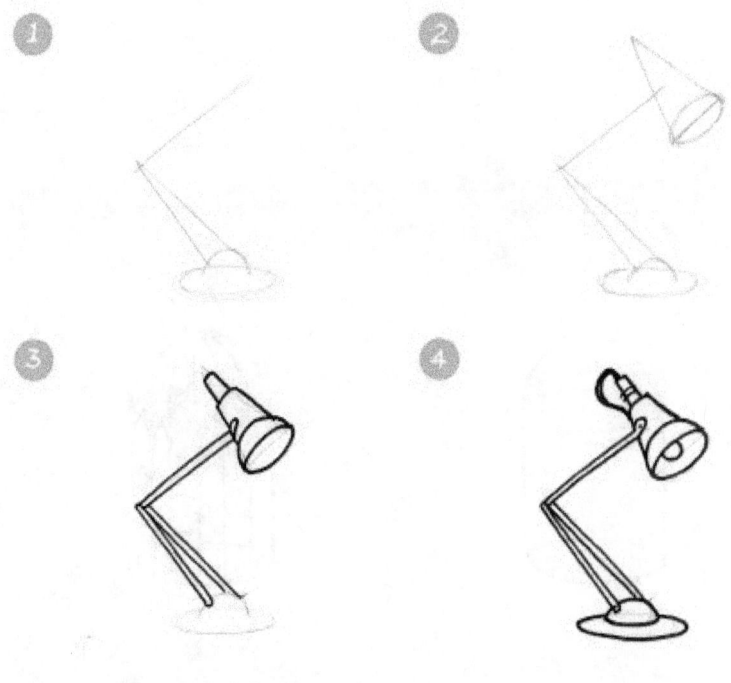

Bird cage

Like any symmetrical object, it's a good idea to start with a vertical foundation line, and use that to help you keep everything the same distance either side of it.

Take your time adding in the vertical lines and then the curved lines around the dome part. It's also nice to add in some detail, according to how ornate you'd like your bird cage to be.

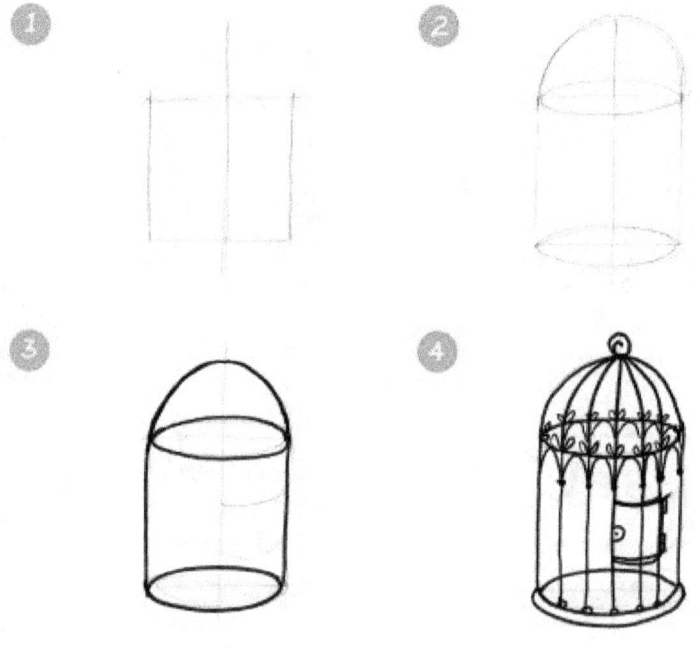

Lava lamp

Lava lamps are so mesmerising to look at! Have a go at this particular shape; once you get the hang of it, you can adapt this to be any shape you like.

My lava lamp sketch here is based on a bit of a 'rocket'-shaped set of foundation lines. Mark in the container part of the lamp in black, and then draw in some gloops and blobs of 'lava' in whatever colour you like. Groovy!

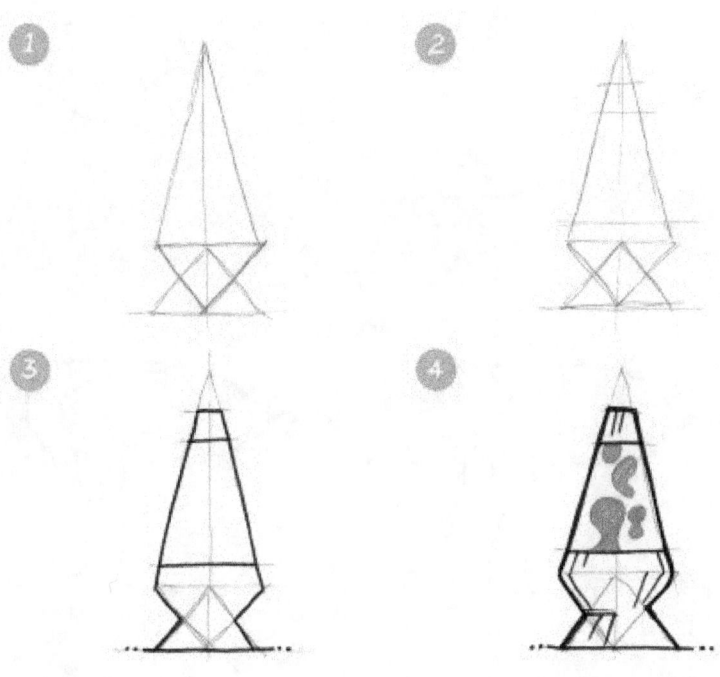

Drill

This drill sketch starts with a horizontal line to mark the centre, and then a rectangle and circle around it, to mark out the space for the head and body of the drill (1). The handle then 'hangs off' these foundation lines.

Finish it off with a few details, like the drill bit itself and a curly line for the finger grip. This pattern also works for 60s space ray guns as well!

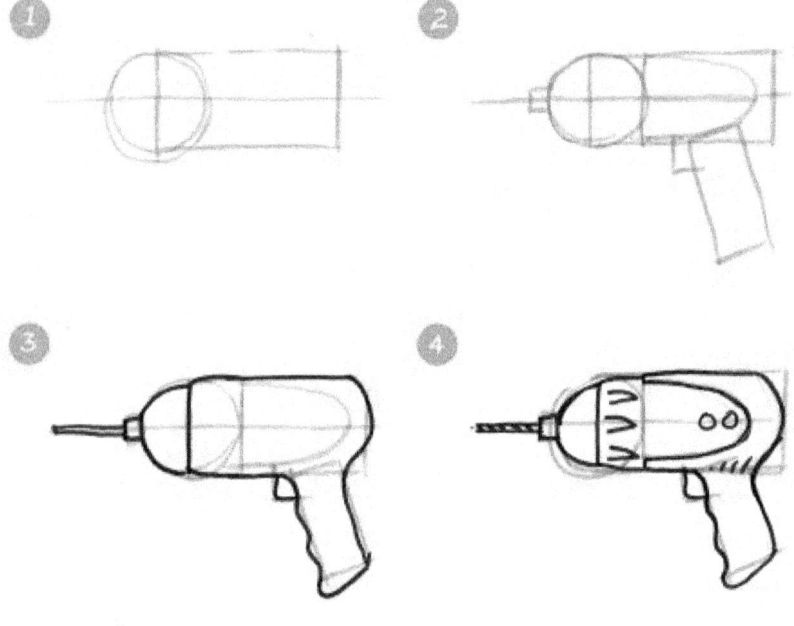

Camera

A camera is one of things that you can draw a basic version and it looks fine, but if you add just a bit of detail in the right way, it can look absolutely smashing!

Use the foundation lines in step 2 to position the lens of your camera (3). Precision is the aim of the game here; once you mark it all in with your black marker, it'll look pretty smart.

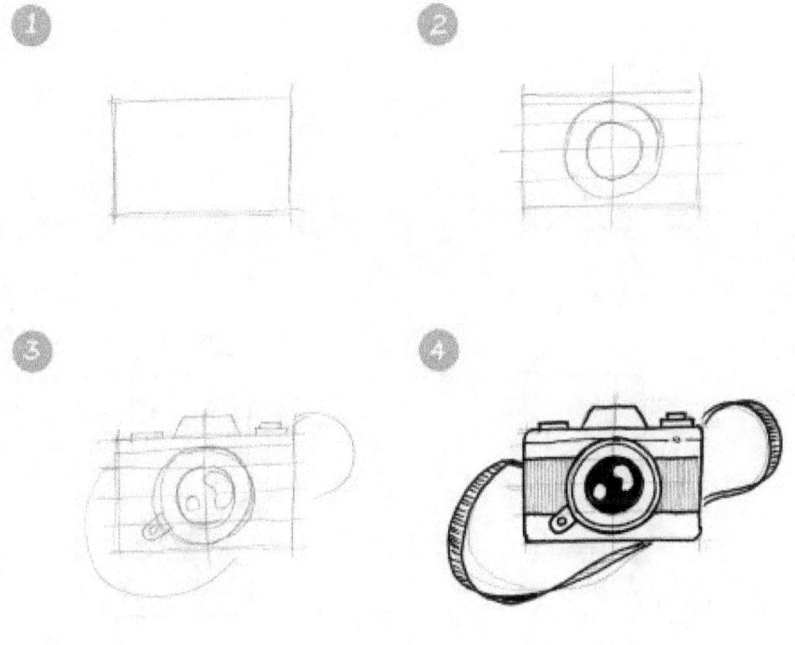

Blender

The overall shape of a blender is easy to master, and the little details can make all the difference. Start with a long vertical line, and draw a tall rectangle either side of it (1).

Sketching in the triangles in step 2 helps you to describe the base and curved shape of the clear part of the blender more confidently. Don't forget to add some details for the lid, the spout, and a dial on the base.

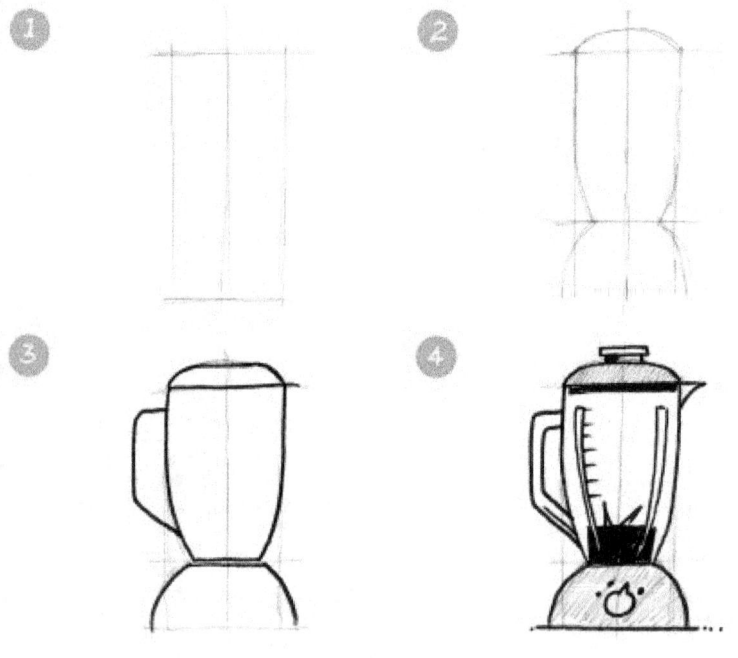

Bed

Sketch a horizontal rectangle, followed by two long diagonal lines extending downward, linked by a narrower rectangle (1). Sketch in some foundation lines for the pillows, the bed covers, the base, and the head of someone in the bed (2). With your black marker, use the foundation lines as your guide to draw in the bed head, bed clothes, base, pillows and head (3). Add a few more details, and you're done!

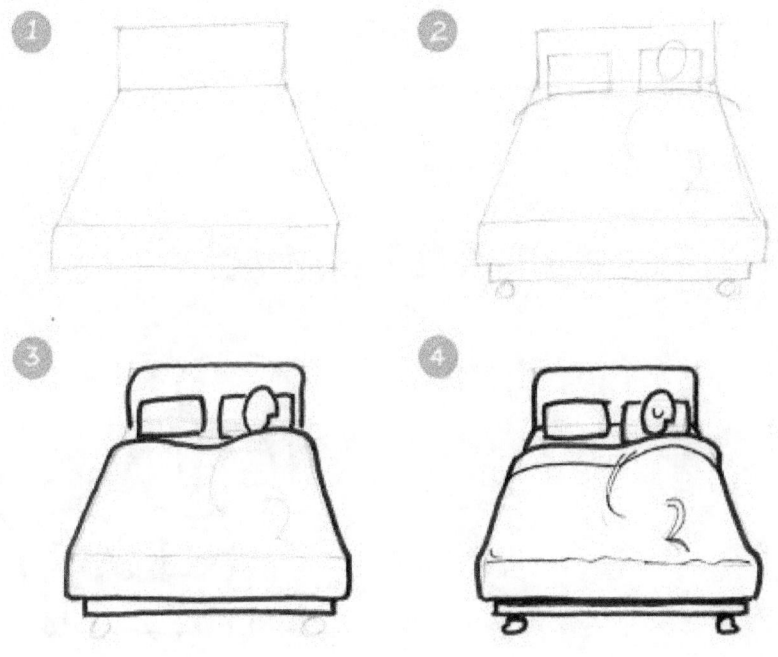

Couches

This sketch uses the same pattern for a single and a two-seater couch. Step 3 is a little tricky, but the illusion you'll get is worth it: sketch some curved lines from the circles inward to that first middle horizontal line, and then a second horizontal line below the first one. Link them with diagonal lines (3). Now you can mark in the couches with your black marker, and accessorise with cushions, cats, or anything else you like.

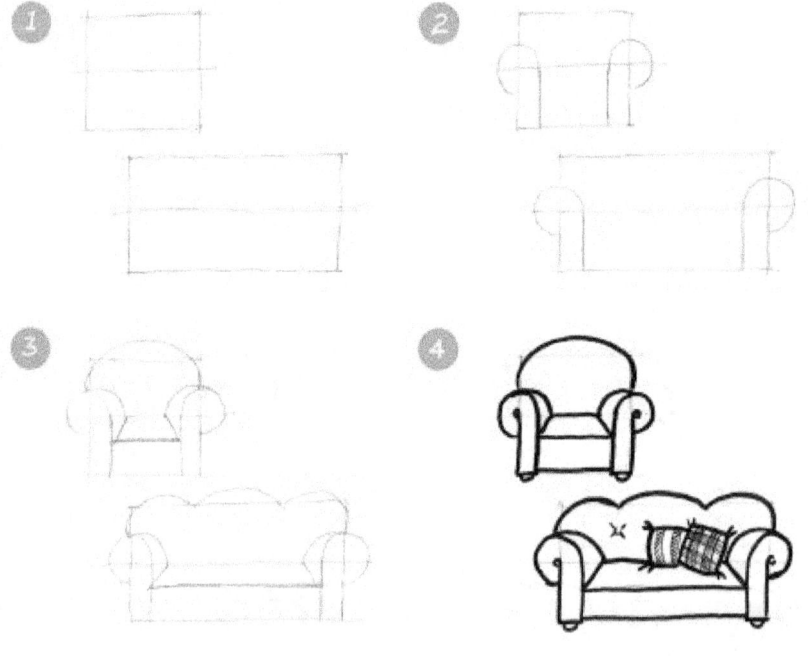

Medicine bottle

This medicine bottle is good practice for any cylindrical object with multiple widths (e.g. binoculars). This one doesn't use a vertical line, so you can get used to the idea of sketching in ovals within shallow rectangle shapes instead. Notice how you can 'stack' ovals as foundation lines to describe different parts like the lid, and to make sure that the curve at the top of the lid matches the curve at the bottom of the lid.

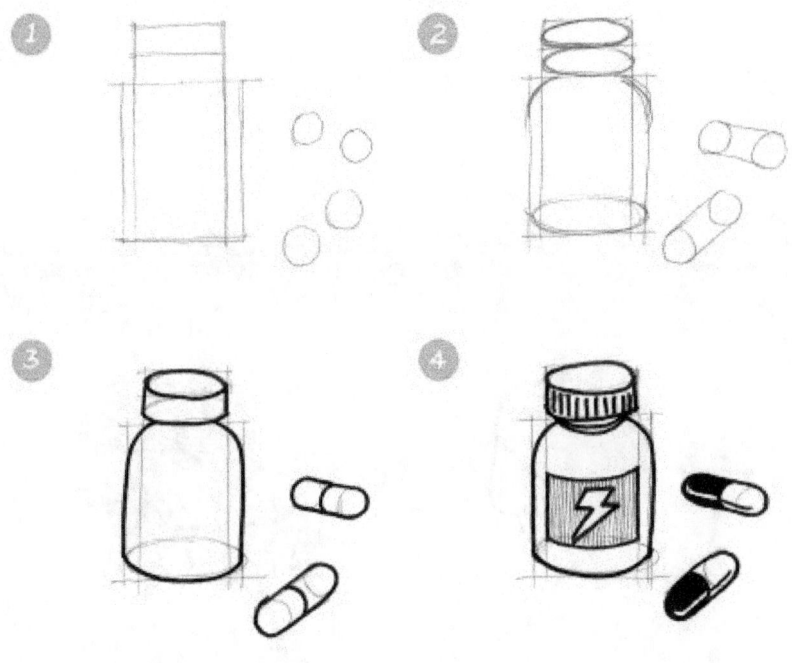

Chair

This isn't any old chair we're drawing here. This is the mid-century style icon Womb Chair, by renowned Finnish American architect and industrial designer Eero Saarinen.

Don't be discouraged if your first attempt doesn't look right; it took me a few attempts to get this, too! Use this one as practice for drawing graceful curved lines around boxy foundation lines.

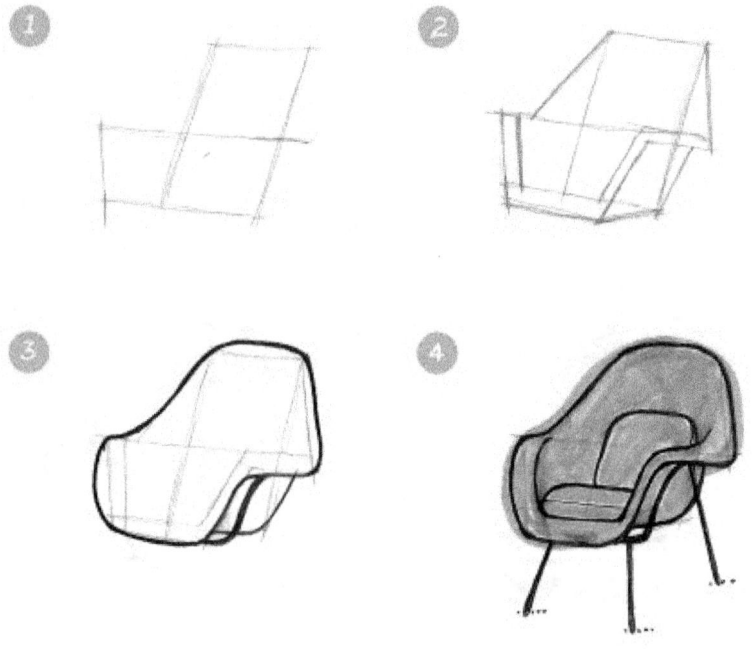

Out and about

From on the ground to in the air, from on the water to under the water, you'll have transport well and truly covered if you master this set of objects.

As you do each of these practice sketches, think about how you might make it your own, customise it, and take it further... and then go ahead and sketch it again your way.

What you'll draw in this section

Bicycle, skateboard, car, rocket, submarine, caravan, cruise ship, sparkplug, moped, parachute, helicopter, airplane, yacht, Viking ship, and a deep sea diver.

Bicycle

You can start sketching a bicycle by sketching two circles for the wheels (1), an equilateral triangle with its left point at the centre of the 'back' wheel, and then another equilateral triangle joined to the first (2). Whew! That's the tricky part over. Ink in the circles and frame in black. If you like, you can always accessorise your bike with a line along the back for a rack, and a basket of goodies from the shop, or a dog, or an elephant... you get the idea.

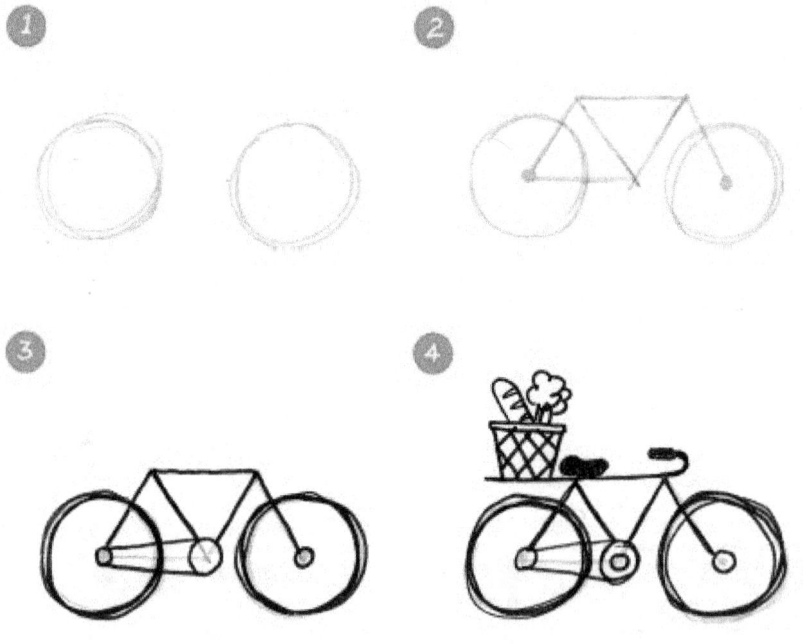

Skateboard

I'm going to go ahead and make a confession: I was never very good on the skateboard. I still have a scar on my foot to prove it!

Start this sketch with a long parallelogram (1). Add a semi-circle at the front, and a rectangle at the back, plus two ovals for wheels (2). Finish it off by inking around the outside, and the cylindrical bits of the wheels (4).

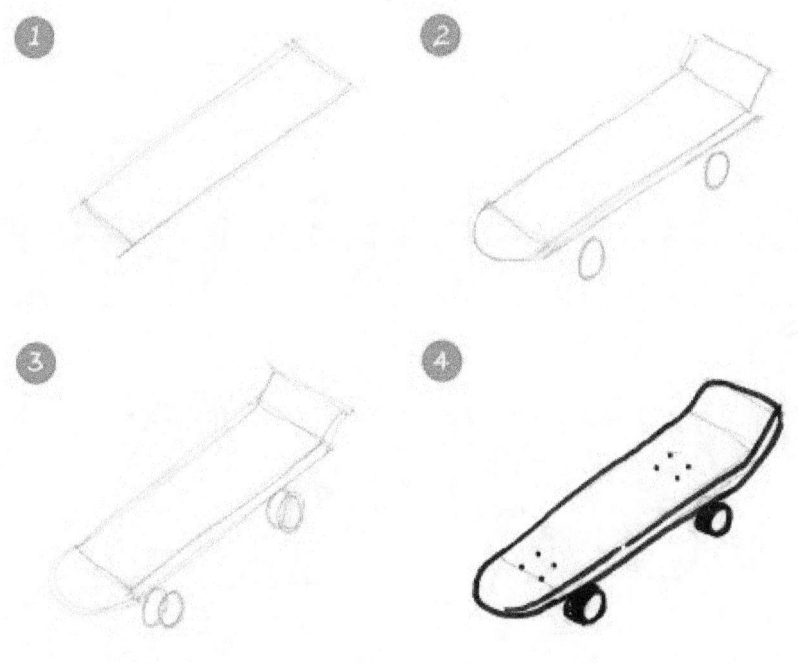

Car

There are probably as many ways to sketch cars as there are people; they have lots of character, and you can even 'pose' them, in some ways. Let's try a simple kind of car that's easy to draw and will give you a satisfying result: a humble hatchback.

Don't be afraid to jazz it up with bumpers and decals on the side.

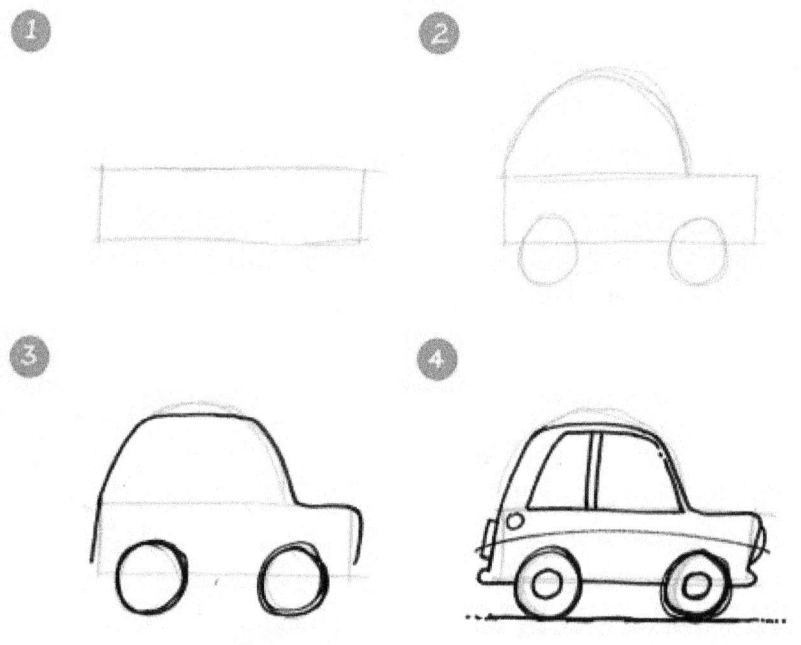

Rocket

Rockets were definitely on high rotation for the things I used to draw as a kid.

Draw two curved lines on either side of the long triangle foundation lines (3). Don't worry if it doesn't look right the first time; that's what foundation lines are for! (2). Add whatever details and character you'd like. One window, or ten? Big retro fins or small modern ones? Take your rocket as far as your imagination will go!

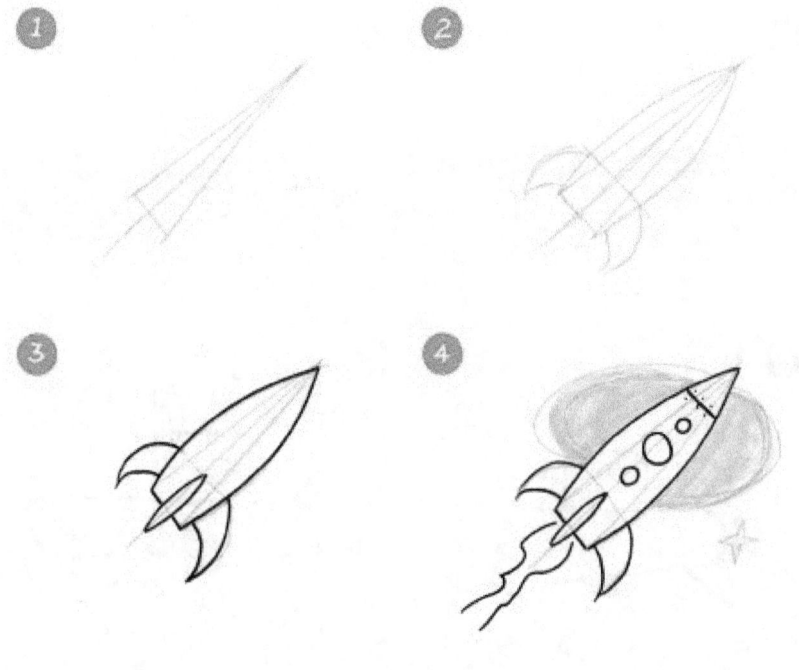

Submarine

Get your submarine going with a long rectangle and triangle at one end for the hull, and a square on top for the sail (1). Add a slight diagonal line along the rectangle (2), with two short diagonal lines for the aft fins.

Now you can ink in the shapes of the hull, sail and fins (3), and add in some details, like a propeller out the back (oops sorry, aft), some portholes, and a periscope. Dive! Dive!

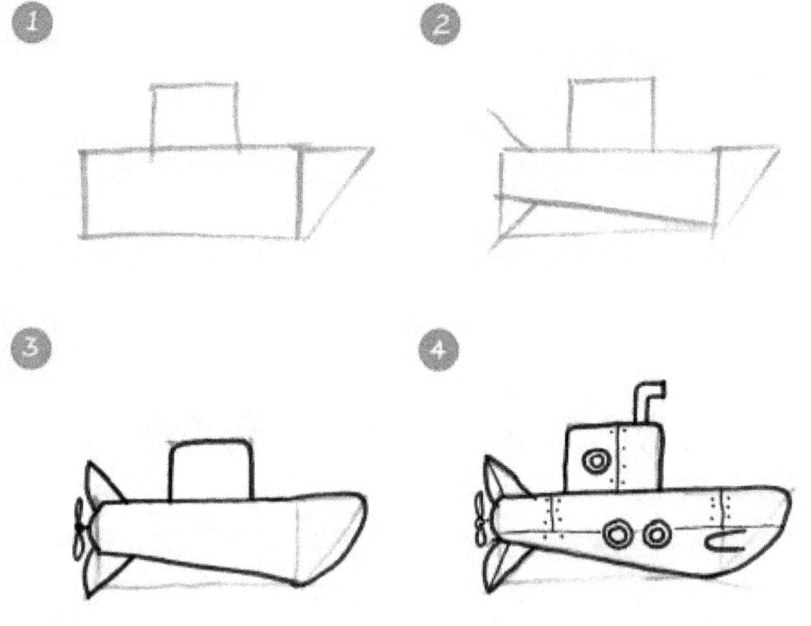

Caravan

Some of the best childhood memories some people have are from spending time touring around places on holiday with a caravan, cooking up the catch from the day's fishing with their tiny kitchens, and bedding down each night using all the funny fold-out beds.

This is a great opportunity to add details to the caravan to make it your own, like a window shade and a curved decal along the side.

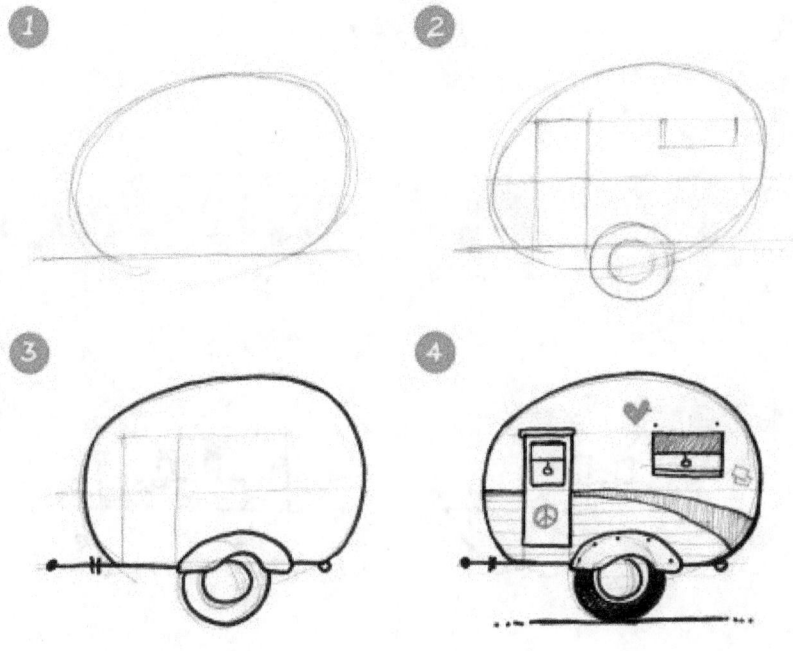

Cruise ship

Everything I learned about relationships I basically learned from Isaac, the bartender on that brilliant 80s show The Love Boat. I've never been on a cruise ship, but I imagine that it's EXACTLY like The Love Boat. Please don't go ruining my dream.

You can probably sketch your cruise ship a bit longer than my one here; sketching it shorter like this makes it somehow more cartoony.

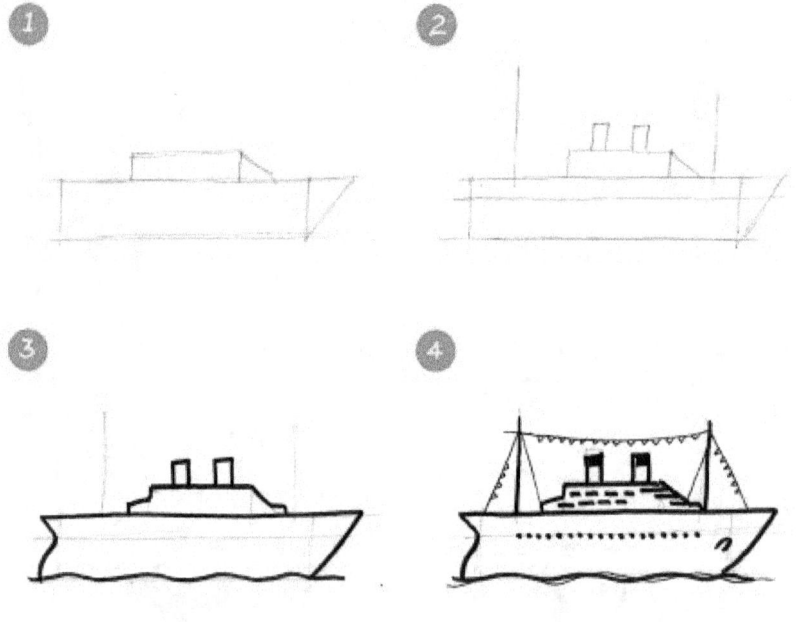

Sparkplug

The cool thing about the sparkplug is the little bit of mechanical detail, so if you pay attention to those bits, it'll really catch your audience's eye. Start with a long diagonal line, sketch some shorter perpendicular lines, and then link up the longest of those shorter lines with the top of the long line to form two triangles (1). If it's hard to work at an angle like this, turn the paper to a 45-degree angle, and sketch your sparkplug straight up and down.

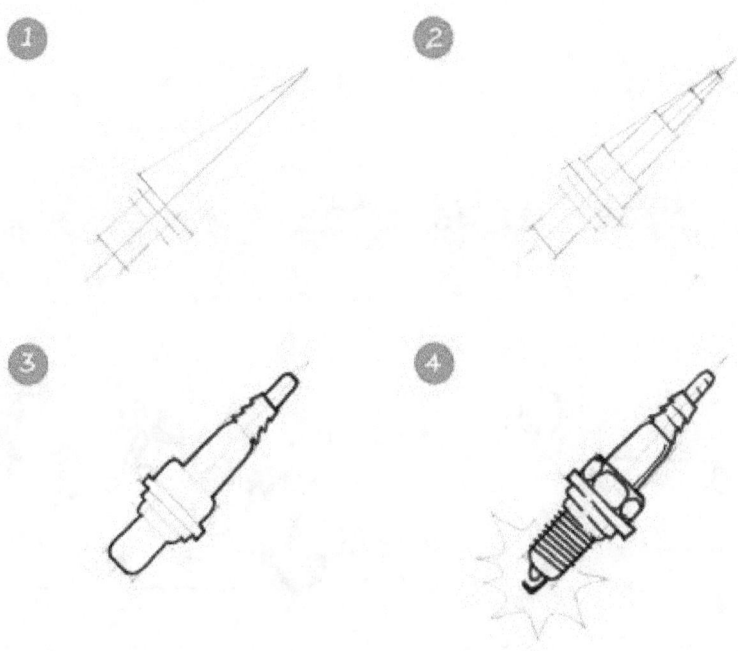

Moped

Mopeds are incredibly popular wherever the roads are really narrow (like most European cities), and wherever there are a lot hipsters and coffee shops to be found. My happy place, basically.

Like a lot of these 4-step practice sketches, your first moped probably won't look right, but sketch a few more, and then they'll look amazing!

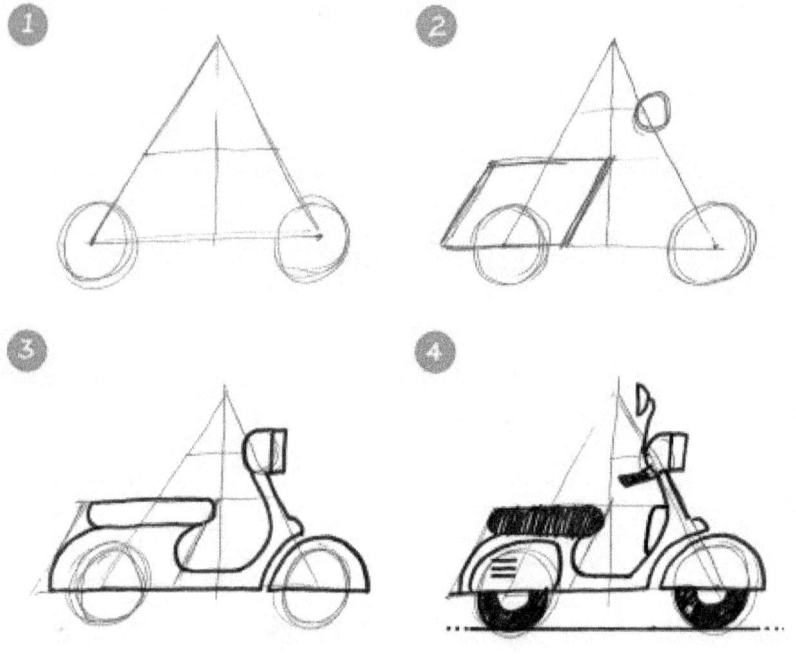

Parachute

Start your parachute sketch with a nice plump oval at a bit of an angle, with two lines descending to a point (1). Sketch a curved line across the oval, and a little figure with its head at the meeting point of the two lines (2).

Use the curved foundation line across the oval as a guide to draw some crescents for the rim of the parachute, with curved lines up to the top edge to show the parachute billowing out.

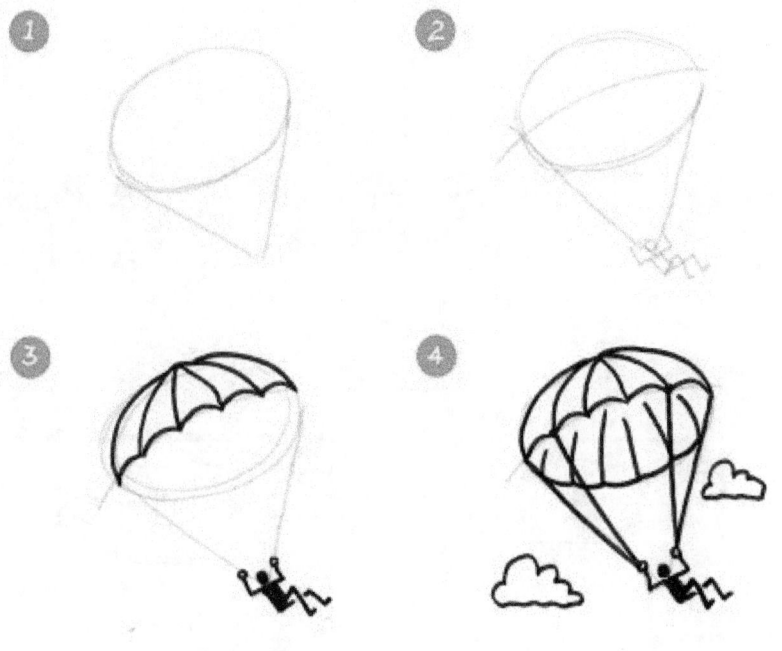

Helicopter

When it comes to sketching helicopters, they're a bit like cars: they can have a lot of personality. You can do sleek long ones like Sikorsky Black Hawks and Bell AH-1 Cobras, or plump cute ones, like the Bell 47 with the bubble canopy. Use the long diagonal line as the 'spine' that everything else hangs off: the tail, the body, the nose, and so on. Finish your helicopter with a bit of detail, like the skids (or wheels) and a whirly top rotor.

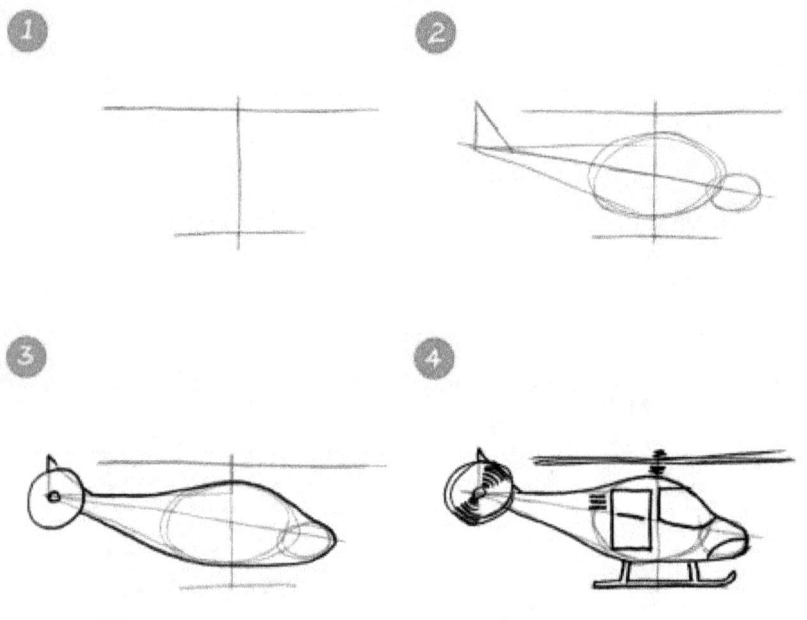

Airplane

Start your airplane by sketching a long narrow rectangle for the
fuselage, and lightly sketch in cross-lines at the half-way and
quarter-way marks (1). Sketch some long triangles in the 'second
quarter', and little triangles in the last 'quarter'. Note how the bottom
little triangle 'sits' on that inner guideline. Mark in the outlines and
dots for windows, and your airplane sketch will really take off! (okay,
no more bad jokes, I promise).

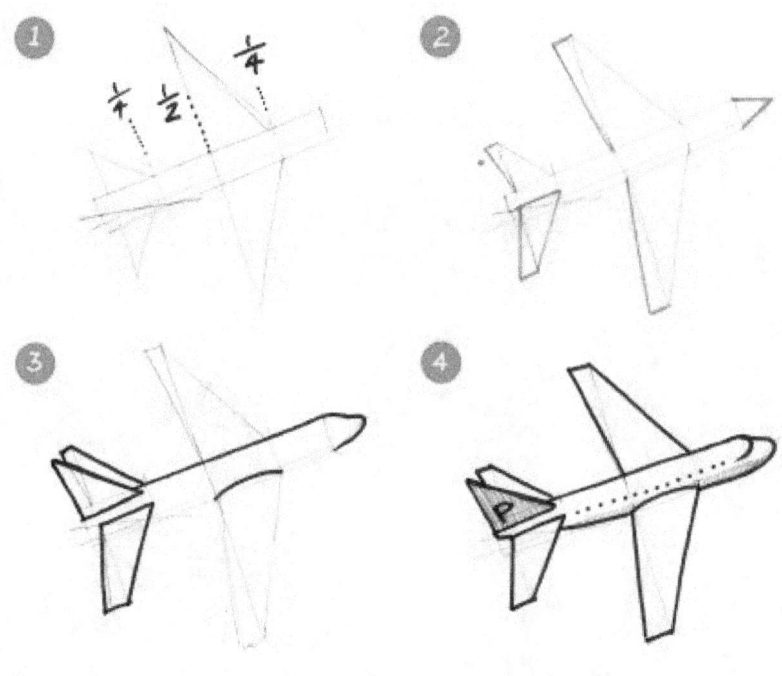

Yacht

Sketching yachts can be really relaxing and rewarding. You can capture some graceful-looking sails and a big swooping spinnaker in just a few lines, and adding a bit of a bird in the air and a reflection in the water just adds to the magic.

I've gone a bit overboard with details in the final frame of this practice sketch, only because I was just having too much fun with it!

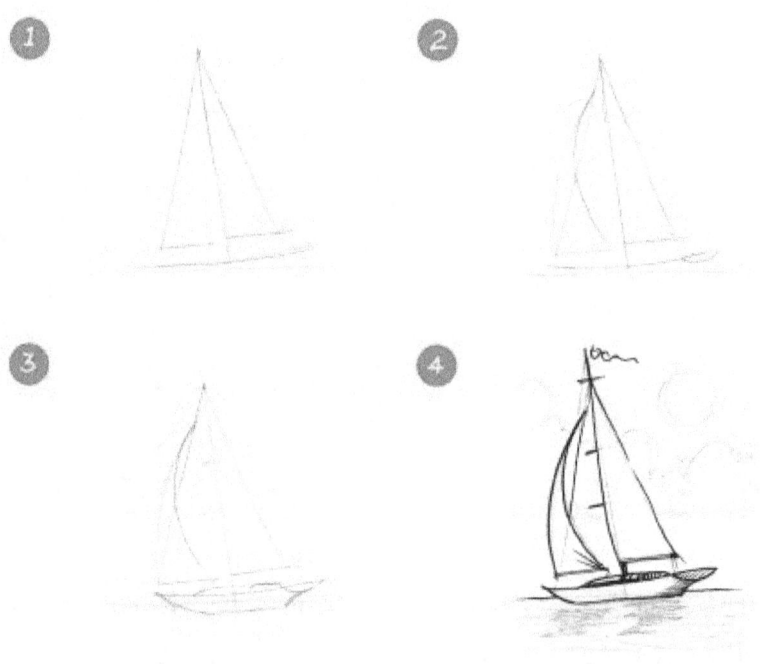

Viking ship

If yachts don't quite take your fancy for life on the high seas, what about a Viking ship then? The circle foundation lines make it look a bit like a car at the start, but they're just there to help you describe the shape of the long hull.

Add a flag, some shields and oars, and any other details that you'd like. Now, you're all set to go pillaging!

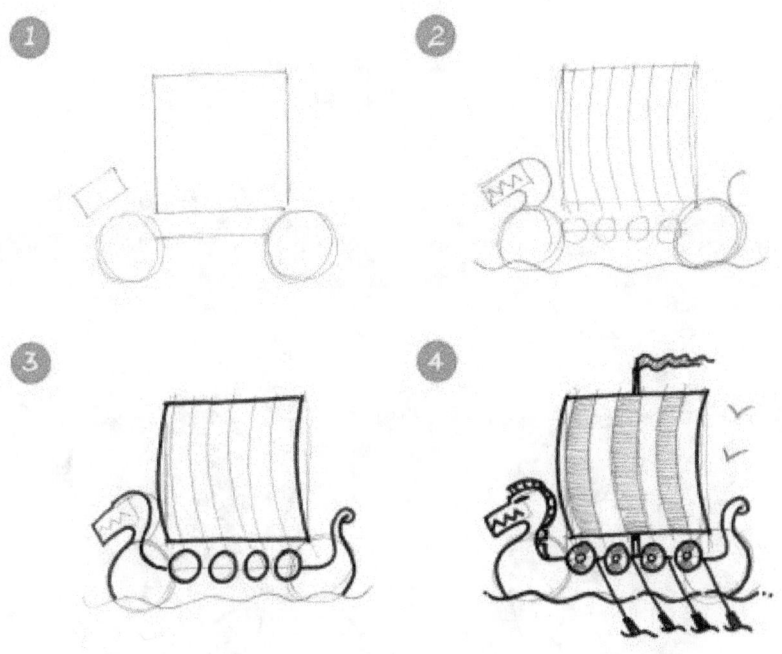

Deep sea diver

Although we've had various diving outfits and contraptions since the early 1400s, it wasn't until the 1820s that diving helmets like this one (in all their steampunk copper glory) came about, invented by Charles and John Deane.

Take your time with the details on this one, and your drawing will come out looking pretty snazzy. Don't forget the air hose, and your diving helmet is set for adventure!

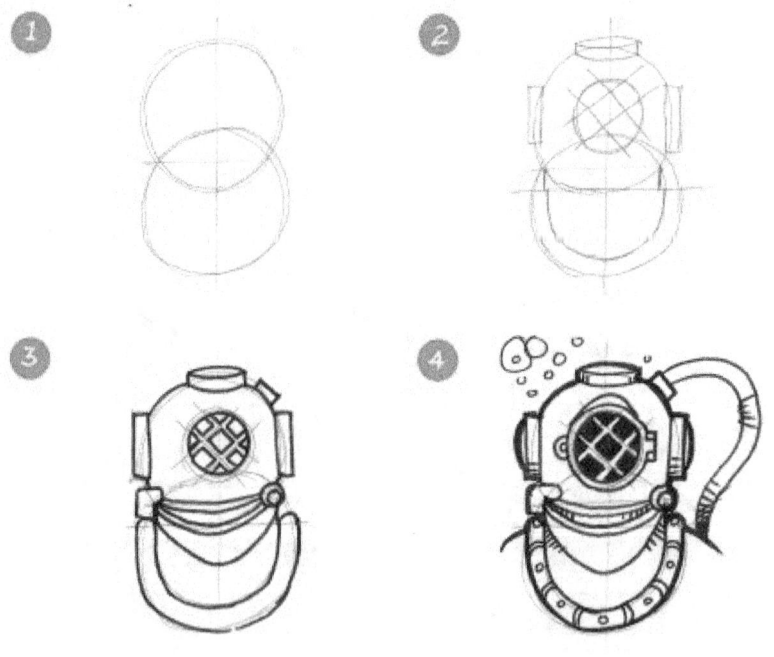

Animals and nature

Having a menagerie of animals in your sketching repertoire is not only fun, but can actually be super useful for visually exploring problems and explaining unfamiliar concepts to others in a really engaging way.

How? Because so many animals also double as character traits, like the slowness of the sloth or tortoise, the speed of the hare, the curiosity of the fox, or the deathly grasp of the dreaded kraken...

What you'll draw in this section

Sea lion, tortoise, hare, horse, shark, panda, cat, kangaroo, sloth, vulture, octopus, fox, seahorse, scorpion, and a kraken.

Sea lion

Why are we drawing a sea lion, and not a seal, you might be wondering? A drawing of a seal can look a bit like a cucumber with eyes if you're not careful, whereas a drawing of a sea lion is a bit easier. Sea lions have ears and nice big flippers, which are more satisfying to draw.

Finish off your seal with a few whiskers, an ear flap, and some lines on the flippers (4). Isn't he adorable?

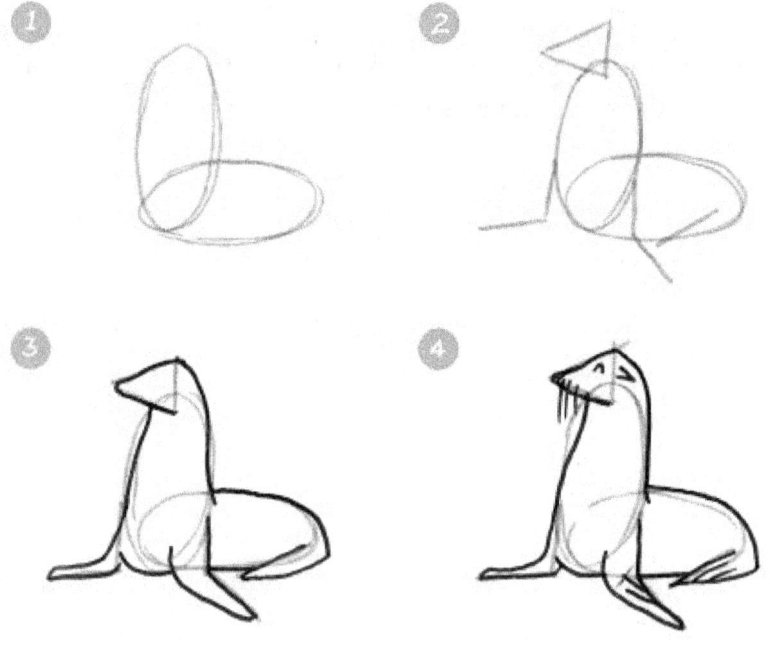

Tortoise

Tortoises might get a bad rap for being slow (especially when racing hares), but back in 1968, a few tortoises were the first living things to fly around the Moon, aboard the Soviet Union's *Zond 5* spacecraft. Why anyone would pack a spaceship with tortoises is beyond me, but apparently, it's true. Maybe they actually came back with superpowers, who knows?

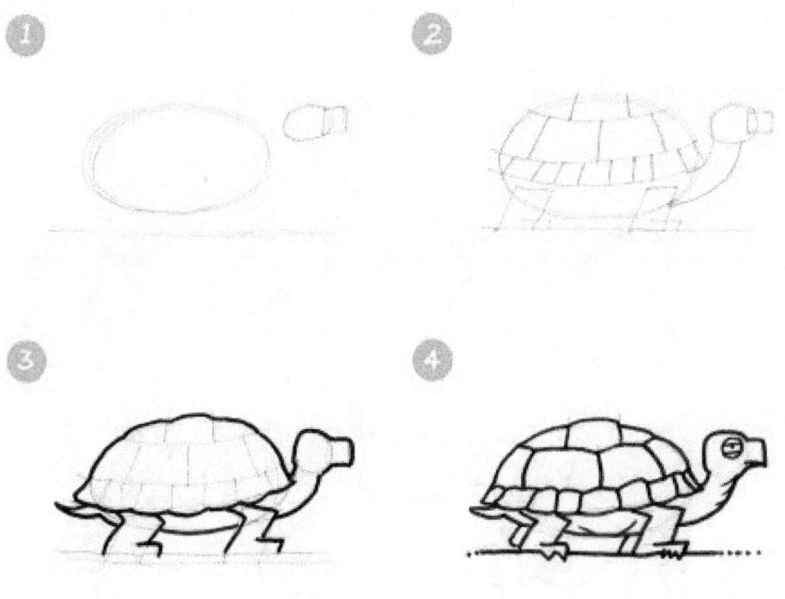

Hare

Hares are a great metaphor for *speed*; they can run up to 70 kilometres (43 miles) an hour! Another fun fact: a male hare is called a jack, a female is called a jill.

Hares have longer ears and limbs than rabbits, so when you're sketching a hare, make sure your foundation lines for the ears (1) and limbs (2) are nice and long. Hares tend to look a bit skinny compared to rabbits too, especially when they're bounding along like this character here.

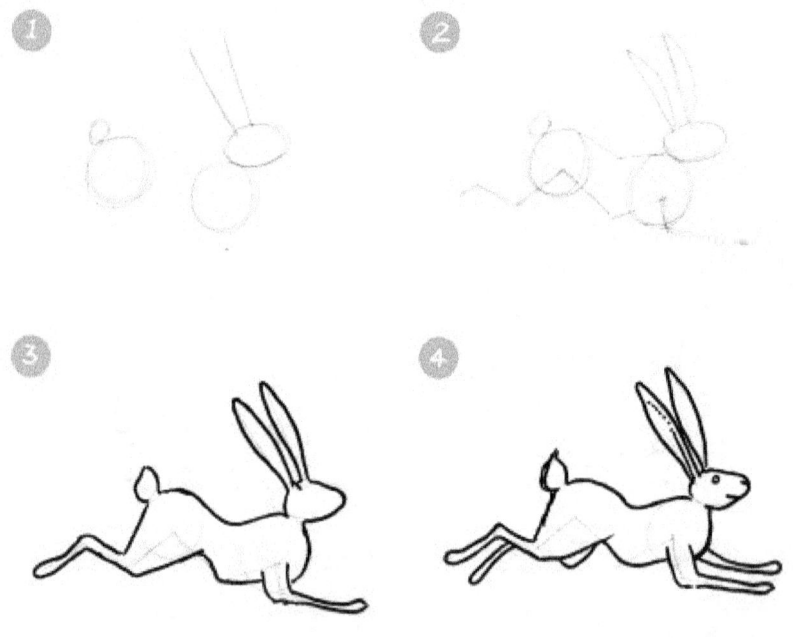

Horse

Horses are a super popular animal to draw, but a lot of people shy away from drawing them because the legs look too tricky to do.... Until now.

These foundation lines give you a nice scaffold to draw the legs in various ways. This horse is in a fairly static pose, but by playing around with the angles of the legs and neck, you can sketch some more dynamic horse poses.

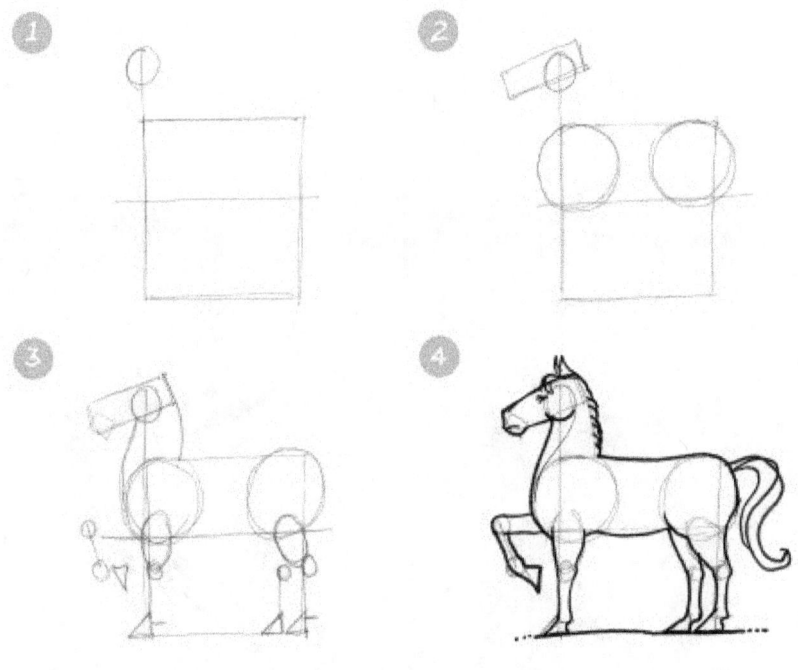

Shark

This sketch starts as a letter D, and ends as a shark! Draw a big letter D that's on a bit of a slope, with two other curved lines inside it (1).

Carefully sketch in the triangles and oval you see in the second step using the inner foundation lines as your guide. Once you do those, you should see your shark coming to life, about to jump right out of the page!

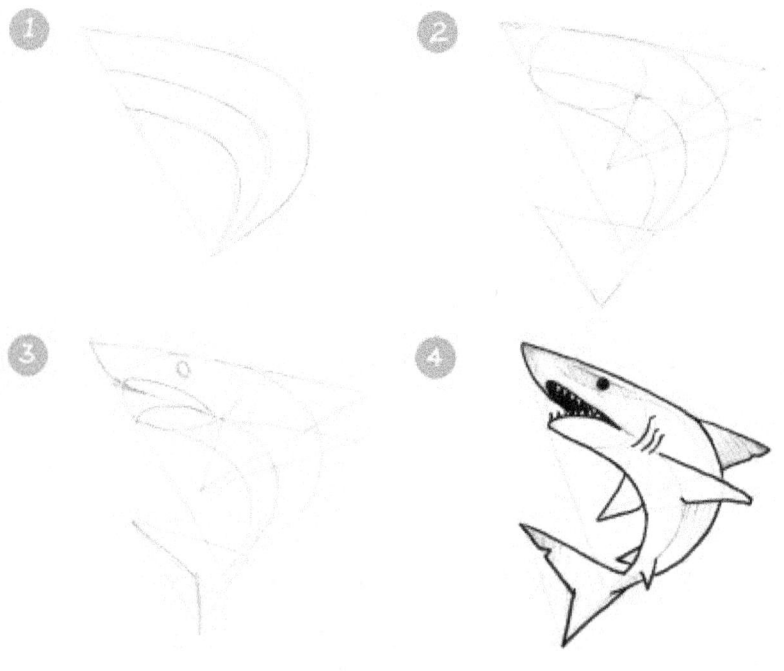

Panda

Good news: pandas are no longer endangered! Although they are still on the 'vulnerable' list, it just goes to show that great positive change is possible when science, political will and local communities come together.

You can mark in the black parts of your panda's fur with your black marker, pencil, or (like I've done here) a dark grey Copic art marker (4).

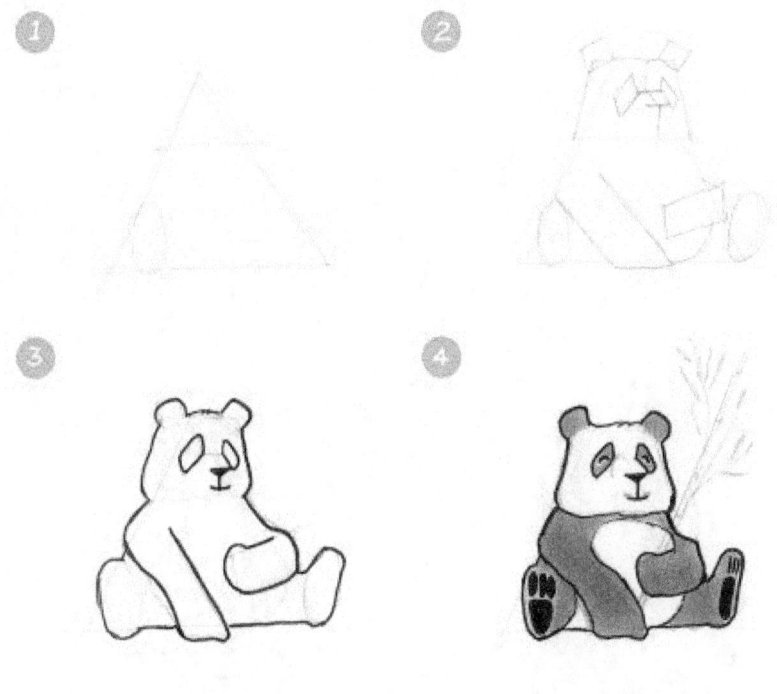

Cat

Often people find it hard to draw cats because the legs can be a bit tricky to get right. Well, here's a way to draw a cat that looks super adorable, where you don't have to worry about drawing legs at all!

This way of drawing cats takes advantage of that beautiful sweeping line they have from head to tail. Use the 'S' line (1) to locate a square at the top for the head, a circle just below it (on the line of the S), and then a larger oval (2).

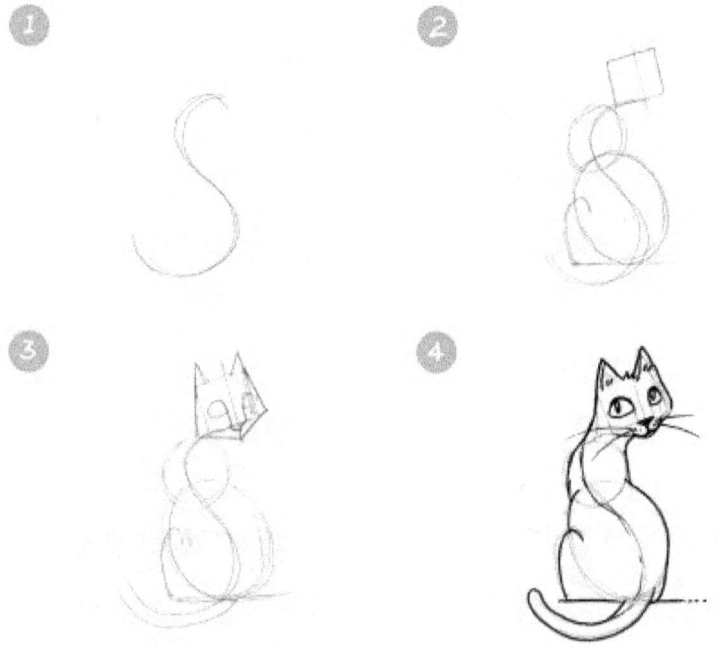

Kangaroo

Kangaroos are amazing animals, plus they're super fun to draw. Like you did with the sea lion, start this sketch with two ovals for the body.

Notice that the lines for the hind legs and the tail are pretty much parallel. These lines together help you get the proportions right (2). Bonza roo you got there, mate!

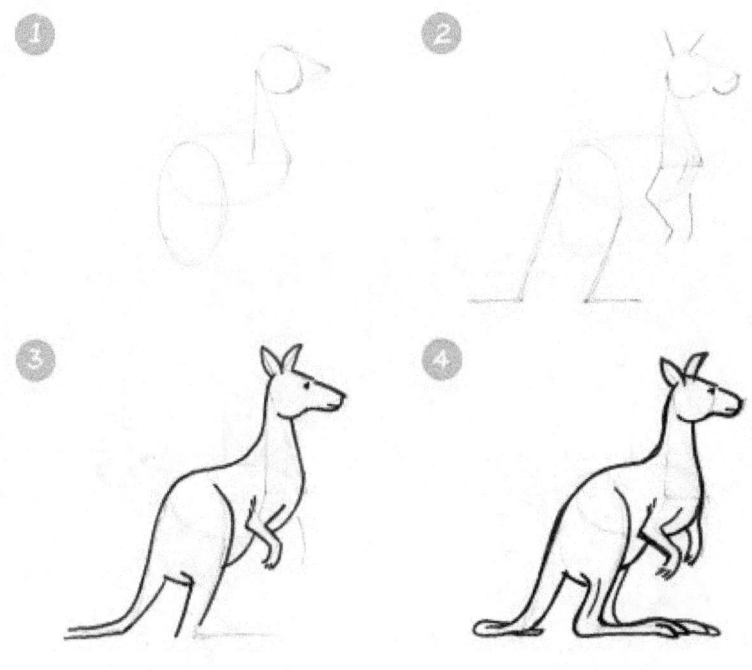

Sloth

Did you know that there's an International Sloth Day, every 28th of October? Take a leaf out of our sleepy friends' lifestyle, and remember to slow down and enjoy the little things in life every once in a while.

The head in my sketch of a sloth is really too big for the body, but I've drawn it bigger to make it easier to draw a nice face on it.

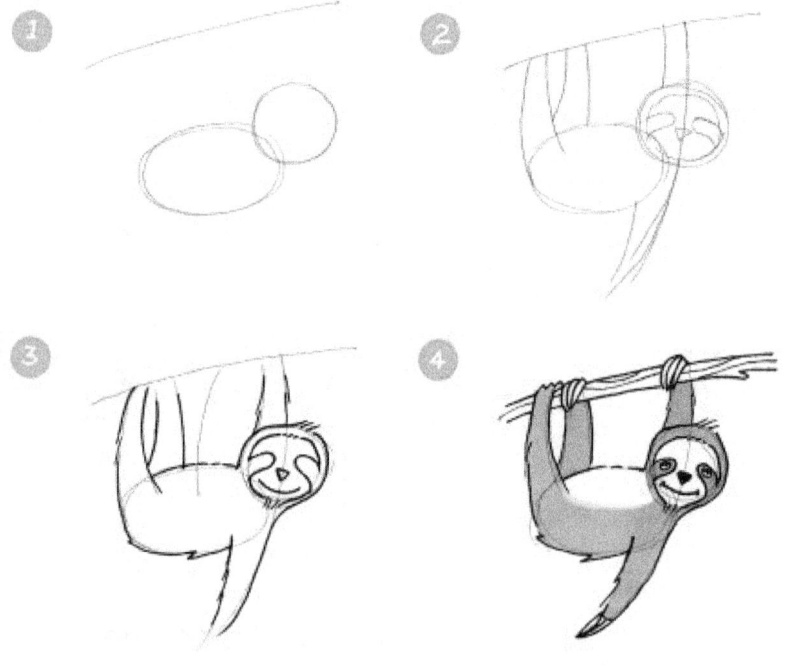

Vulture

Nothing evokes a sense of impending doom like a bunch of circling vultures! Which is a bit of a shame, because they're actually a big help in the wild: as 'Nature's Clean-up Crew', their scavenging helps to prevent the spread of diseases, such as rabies and tuberculosis.

It's always nice to accessorise your vulture at the end. Some assorted skulls, failed exams or stalled projects should do the trick.

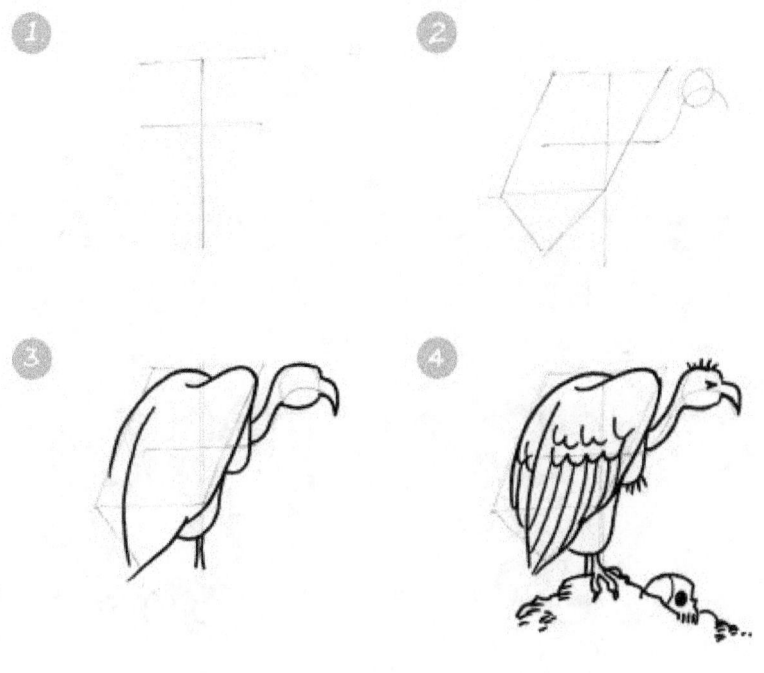

Octopus

Let's get one thing straight: octopuses are incredibly smart. Like chimpanzees, dolphins and crows, they've been observed using tools.

Have some fun filling the larger circle with curly lines radiating out from that little square (2). Don't worry if it gets messy, you might have to sketch this one a few times to get a feel for how much space each tentacle will take up.

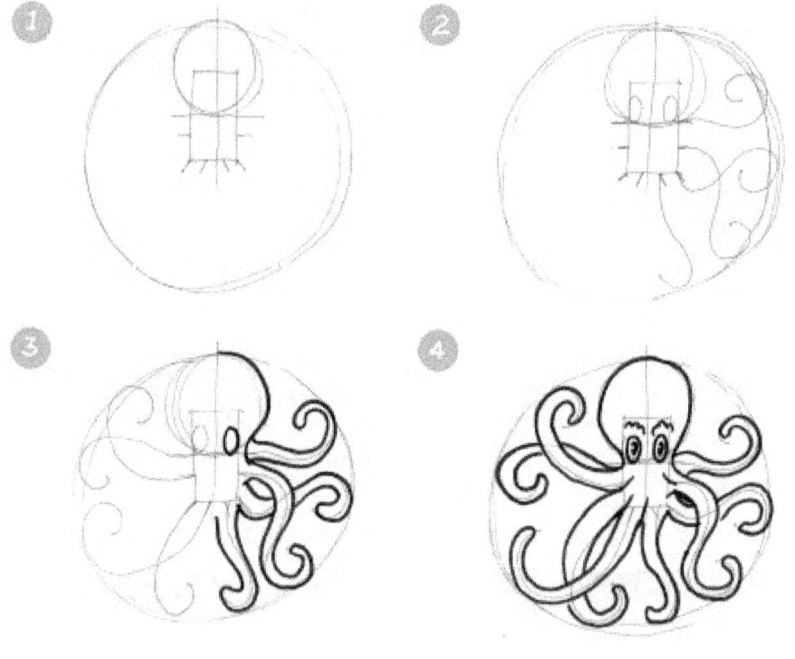

Fox

How cute is this little guy? Foxes are note only pretty cute, but curious too, which is why I like to show this coming through in the sketch's character you see here.

Start with a fairly regular 'mammal' base: a rectangle for the body, a square for the main part of the head, and a line for the tail (1). You can make your fox look more like a fox (and not a dog), by adding a nice bushy tail, and darkening the feet and ears (4).

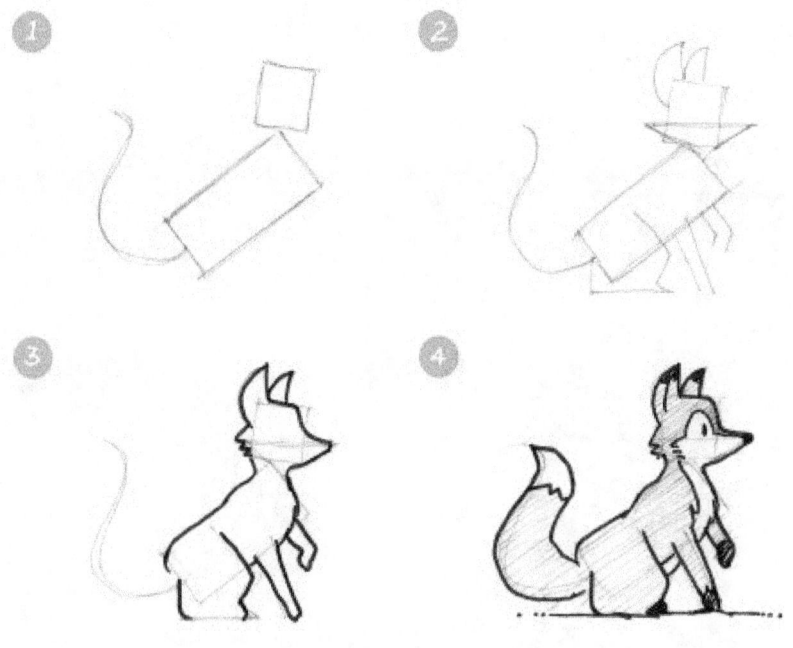

Seahorse

Seahorses have to be amongst some of the most stunning creatures around, and you can have tons of fun drawing these lovely animals using this technique.

Start with a single capital 'S' and then a slightly smaller backwards 'S' (1). That'll become the overall shape of your seahorse sketch. Finish off your sketch with little scallop-shaped lines around the edge, and don't forget the fin at the back!

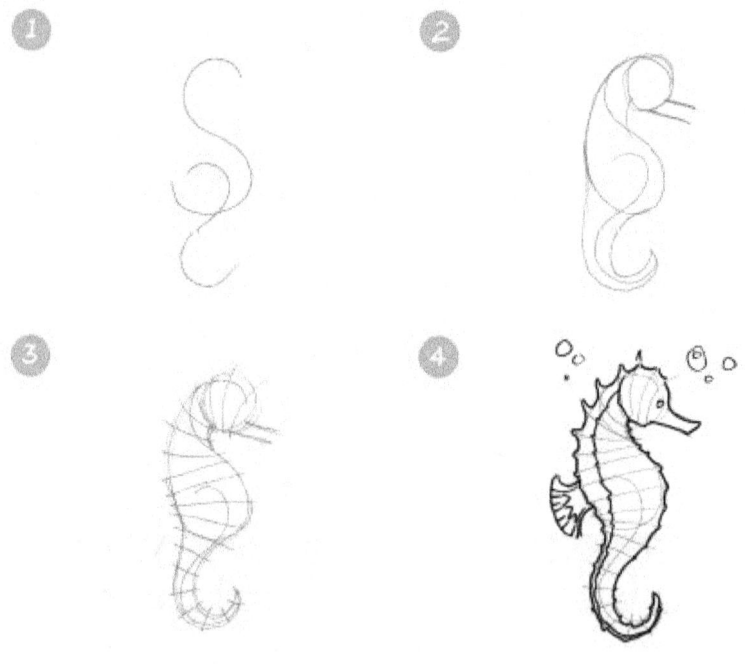

Scorpion

Scorpions can be pretty scary to look at, but very cool to draw. Paying attention to drawing each part of the scorpion makes the end result a whole lot more satisfying.

Start with three curved lines to describe where the body, tail, and the two front nippers will go (1). Describe the head and body as three circles, and the tail as five smaller circles with an extra one at the very end. That last one is actually called the telson, where the stinger goes.

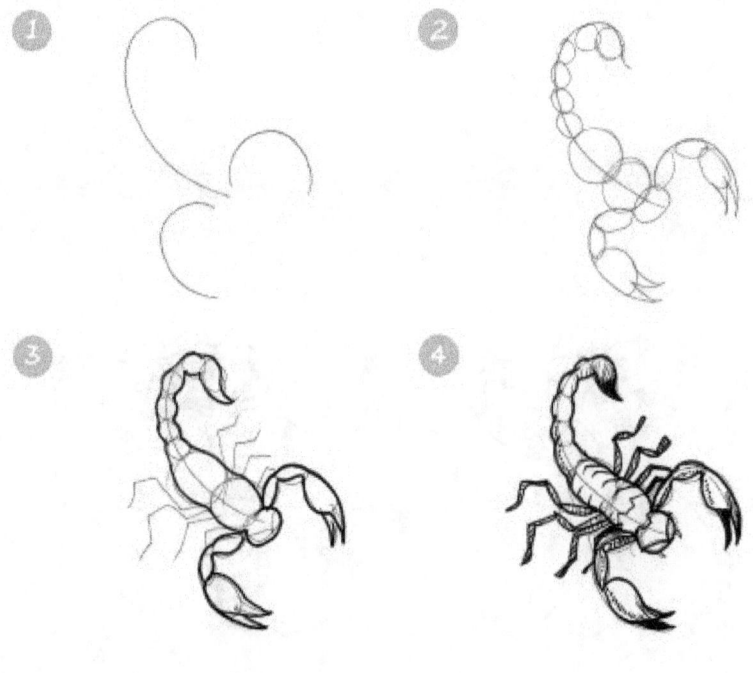

Kraken

Probably the best request I've ever had for a 4-step practice sketch (and probably the hardest) is this: a kraken!

Use the horizontal line of the sea, the triangle-ish shape of the ship and the almond shape of the kraken's body to plot out the main areas of this drawing. Be ready to do this one a few times, as getting all those tentacles to look right takes some practice. But stick with it, because before you know it: Avast! There be the kraken!

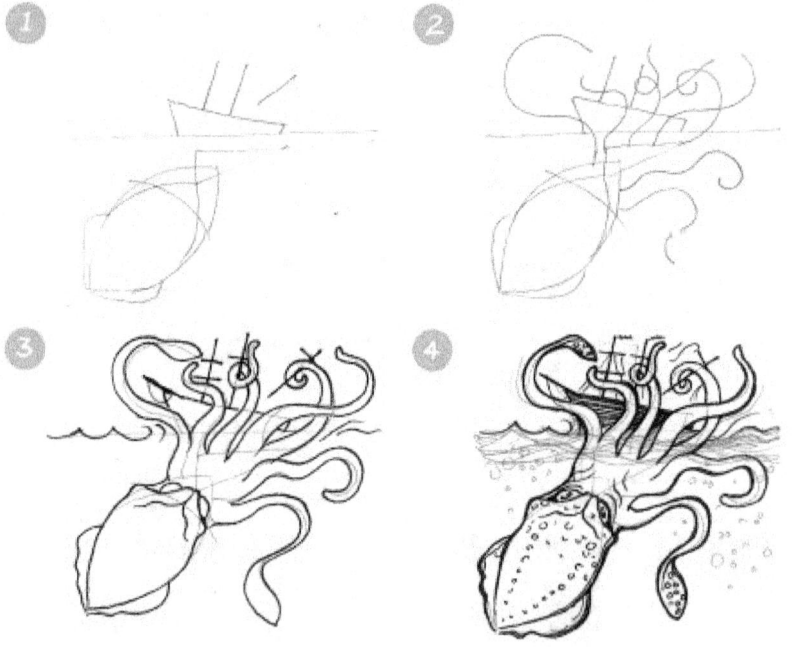

Food and drink

This section was so much fun putting together, and reminded me of the sheer variety of food and drink that we have.

Is your favourite food included here? If not, make sure you have a go at sketching whatever that might be, using the same method: break it down into simple geometric shapes first as foundation lines, and then draw in black over those foundation lines.

What you'll draw in this section

Donut, cold drink, apple core, dinner plate, pineapple, soft drink can, cupcakes, cocktail drinks, sandwich, ice cream, broccoli, bowl of fruit, ramen, sushi, and a chocolate bar.

Donut

Let's start this section with an easy one: a donut. This gives you practice at sketching circles, and thinking about proportion of one circle within another.

Dress up your donut with sprinkles or other tasty accompaniments. I've used little rectangles here, that look like chunky sprinkles, but you can also use small circles, or little spirals, flowers, faces, kittens' faces... whatever takes your fancy!

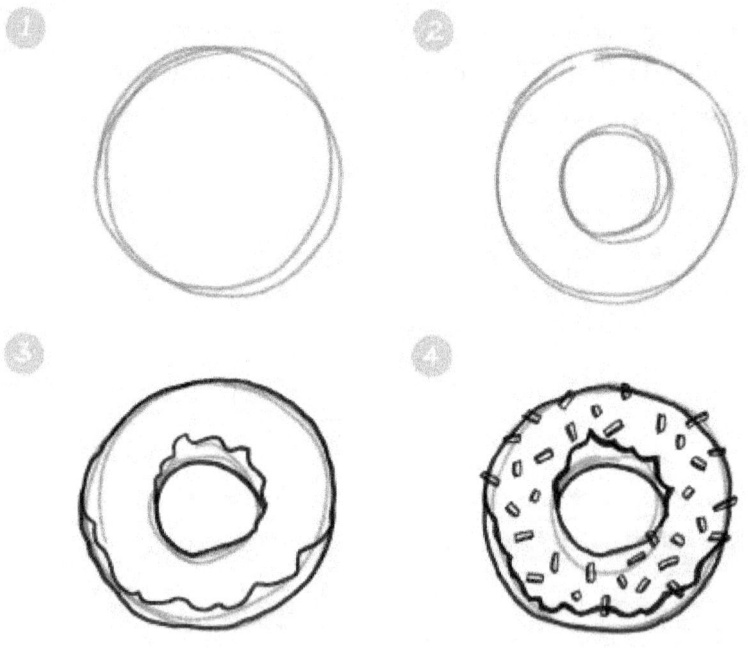

Cold drink

This is another sketch that – just like the donut – is good for practicing turning simple shapes into attractive objects. Take your time with that diagonal line, just kissing the top corner on its way out, as well the circle for the garnish (a slice of lime, perhaps?), and the small squares for the ice cubes (2).

You might like to try changing up the garnish from a slice of lime to a small umbrella. Cheers!

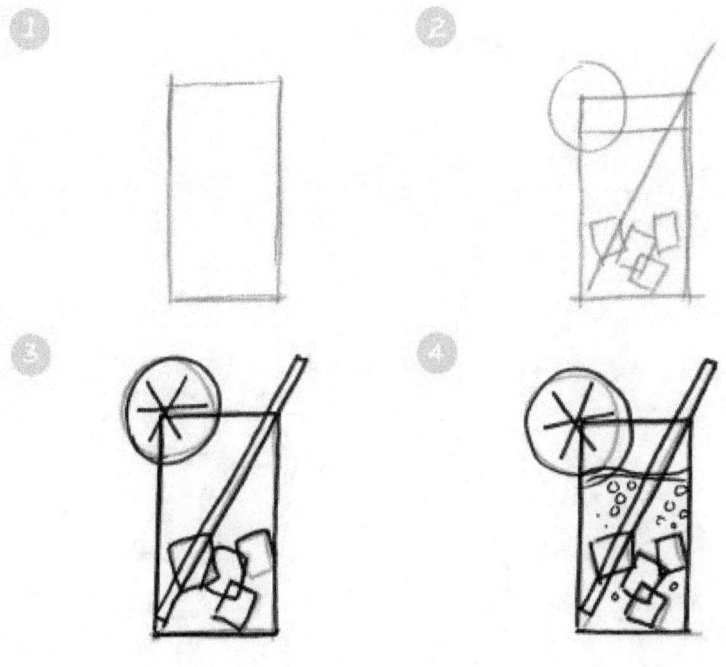

Apple core

Sketching an apple core is surprisingly easy once you break it down into these basic geometric shapes.

Sketch two semicircles with a bit of gap between them (1), and then join up that gap with two perpendicular lines. Ink in two lines of crescents along the straight edges of the semicircles; these are the bit marks from someone who's eaten the apple. Finish it off by drawing curves around the outside, the stalk, and an exposed seed or two.

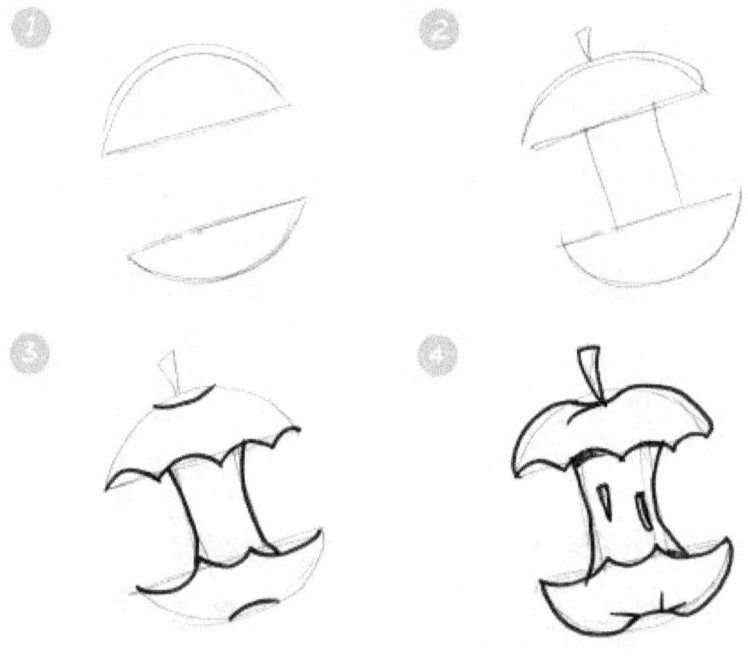

Dinner plate

This particular sketch is definitely a 'sketching 101' exercise! Start by drawing '101', but make sure the 'zero' is nice and round (1).

This dinner plate is actually a nice metaphor for anything that you 'want to make a meal of', i.e. deal with in some way. For example, by sketching a particular problem as the 'meal', you can frame it in a way that looks like it's ready to tackle.

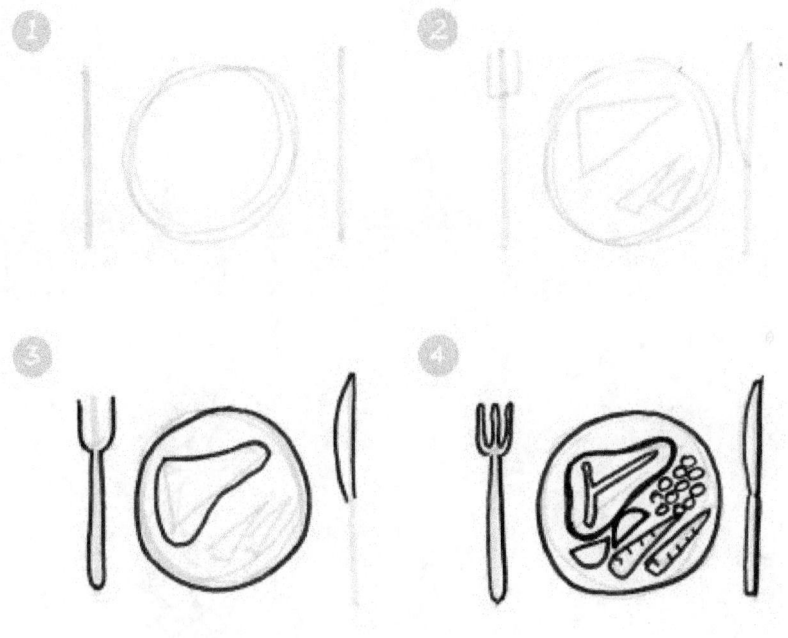

Pineapple

When European explorers first stumbled upon this amazing fruit in South America, they called it 'pineapple' because it looks like a pine cone. The pineapple fruit is actually a whole lot of separate 'berries' fused together as one. Which is sort of useful to think about when sketching one.

The grid of diagonal lines helps you keep those 'berries' in nice lines, which is pretty satisfying.

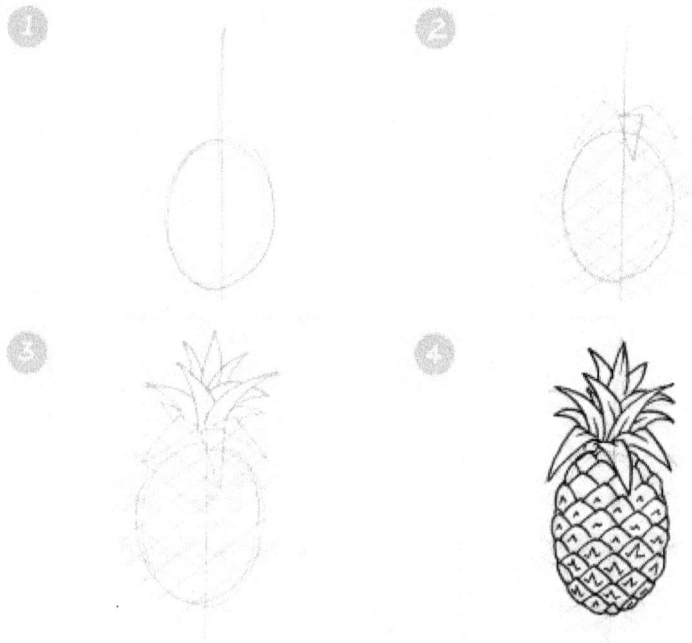

Soft drink can

Drawing a soft drink can (or soda can) is good practice for lining up some nice precise oval shapes. The thing that will make your sketch better than just a regular cylinder is making the top rim a bit smaller than the rest of the cylinder, just like the real thing.

Try turning the paper at an angle and then sketching the can straight up and down, so that then it'll be at an angle when you're done.

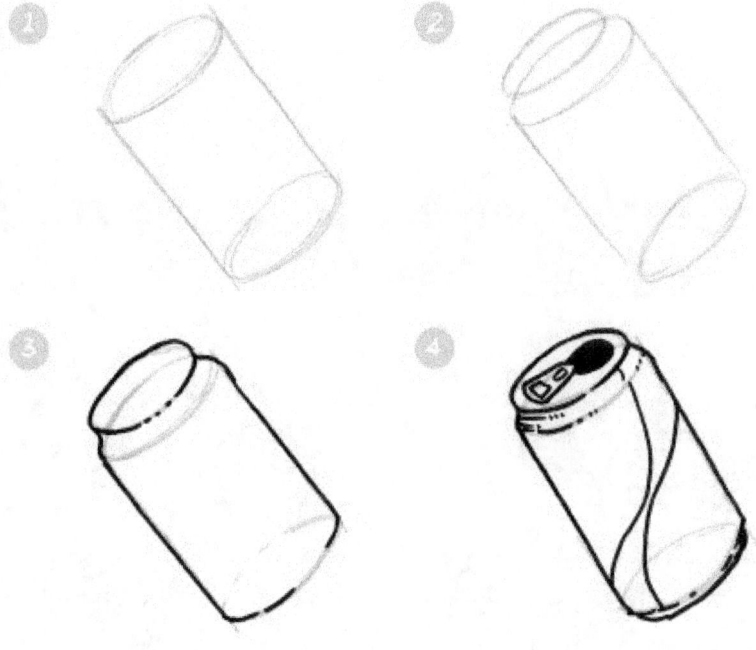

Cupcakes

Cupcakes are nice and easy to draw, and with a little bit more effort you can bring in some nice-looking detail, like the swirl of frosting on top, or the crinkly feeling of the paper cup.

I've drawn two different cupcakes here, to start you thinking about the variety you can bring to a cupcake sketch. Take the opportunity to add some cool details, like a maraschino cherry, or even some cute little faces!

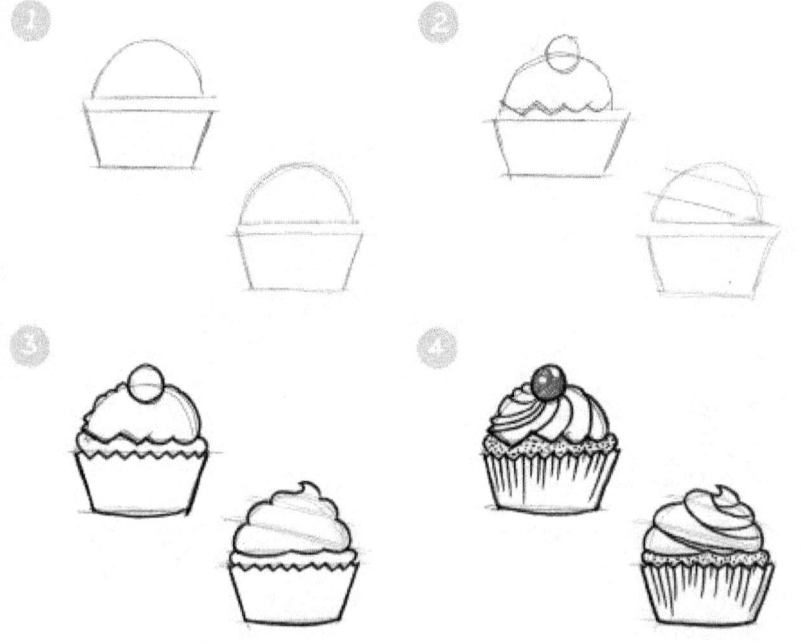

Cocktail drinks

Adding a cocktail drink to any drawing – adding a cocktail drink to anything, really – is bound to give it an extra dash of class. There are two patterns of glass here to choose from; for both of them, start with a vertical line to help you keep them symmetrical.

Remember: you can draw several oval foundation lines on top of each other to help get to one that looks 'right'; they'll visually fade away once you add in your final black line.

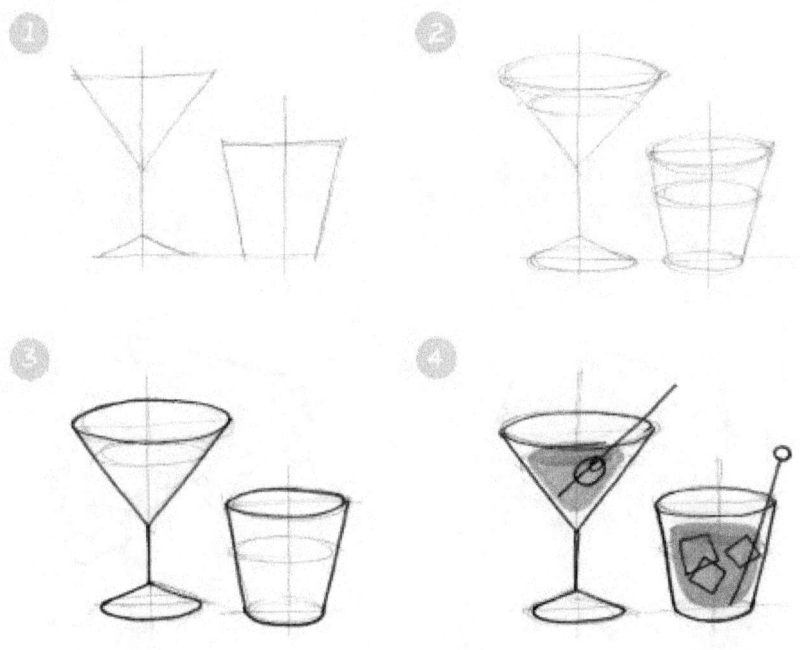

Sandwich

The sandwich was indeed invented by Lord Sandwich, but history has recorded the *way* it was invented in slightly different ways.

Popular myth has it that he never left the gambling table long enough to eat, and had servants bring him some salt beef between two slices of toasted bread to sustain him. Others would order "the same as Sandwich!", which then became 'the sandwich'.

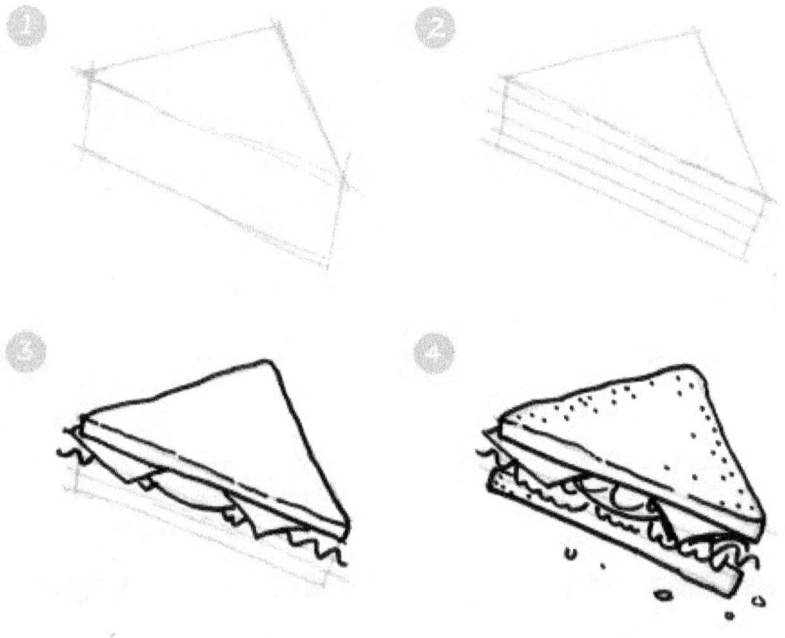

Ice cream

Whether served in a cone or on a stick, ice cream is a fun and tasty thing to add to your sketchy repertoire.

The foundation lines for an ice cream cone are simply a triangle with a circle nestled on top of it, and then another short triangle on top of that circle. For the ice cream on a stick, a long rectangle with a smaller long rectangle at the base is all you need (1).

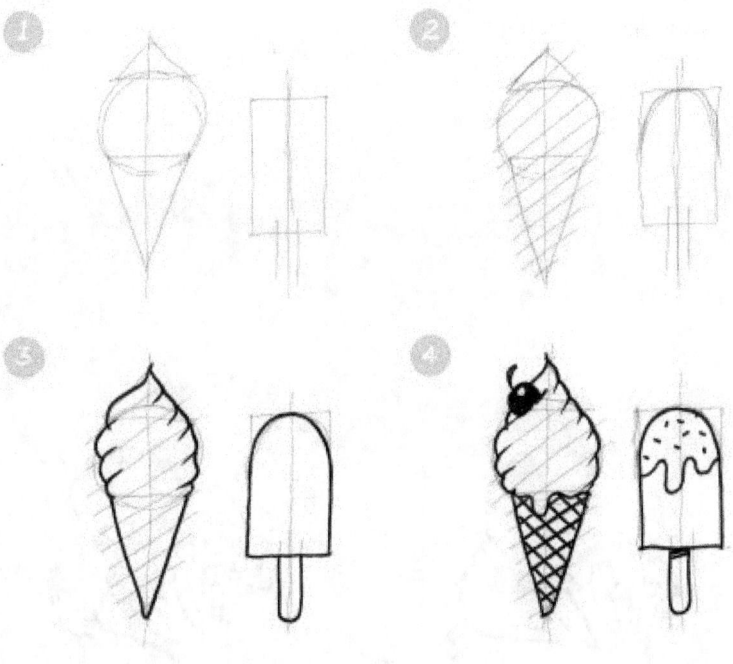

Broccoli

Start your broccoli sketch with a few circles of different sizes, overlapping together (1). Next, add some branched foundation lines all connecting to a square, making it look a bit like a basket with several balloons attached (2).

Add in an oval shape at the bottom to make it look like this broccoli bunch has been cut. This, plus sketching it an angle (rather than straight up and down), helps to make your sketch look more like broccoli, and less like a big tree.

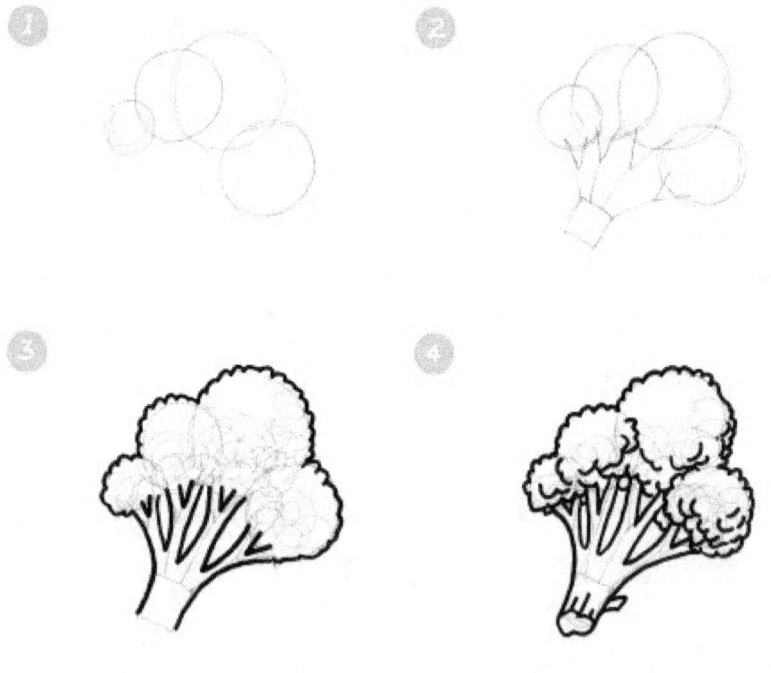

Bowl of fruit

If you rush through this sketch of a bowl of fruit, the contents of the bowl might come out looking more like chunky dog food than actual pieces of fruit, so take your time with this one. And don't worry if your ovals and semi-circles are a bit wobbly. The beauty of foundation lines is that you can go around a few times to get the shape looking a bit better, and by the time you add black over the top, all those multiple lines will blend into one.

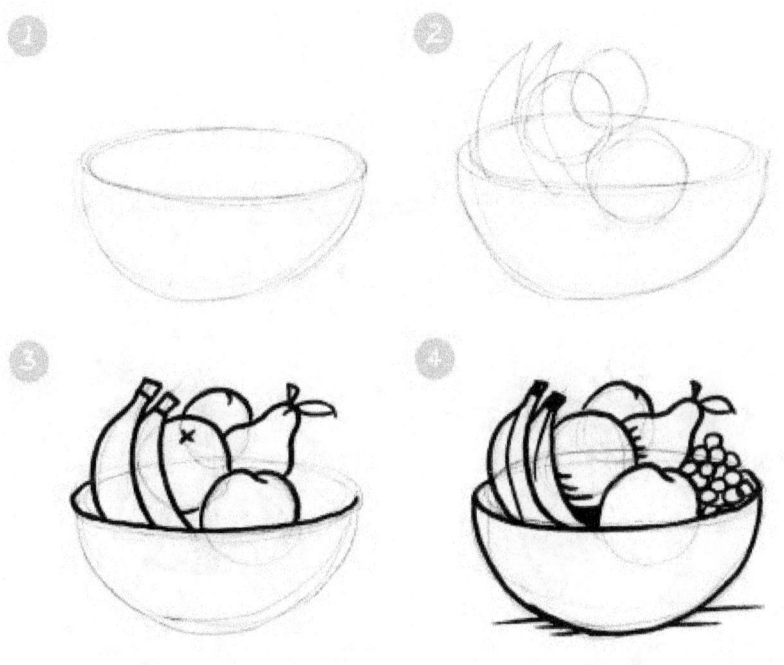

Ramen

While we're sketching bowls, this is a great opportunity to sketch a bowl of yummy ramen.

The trick with this one is getting a feel for the right level of detail to show inside the bowl, like an egg, and that funny pink spiral thingie. Notice that the noodles are carefully-drawn wavy lines, rather than hurried scribbles.

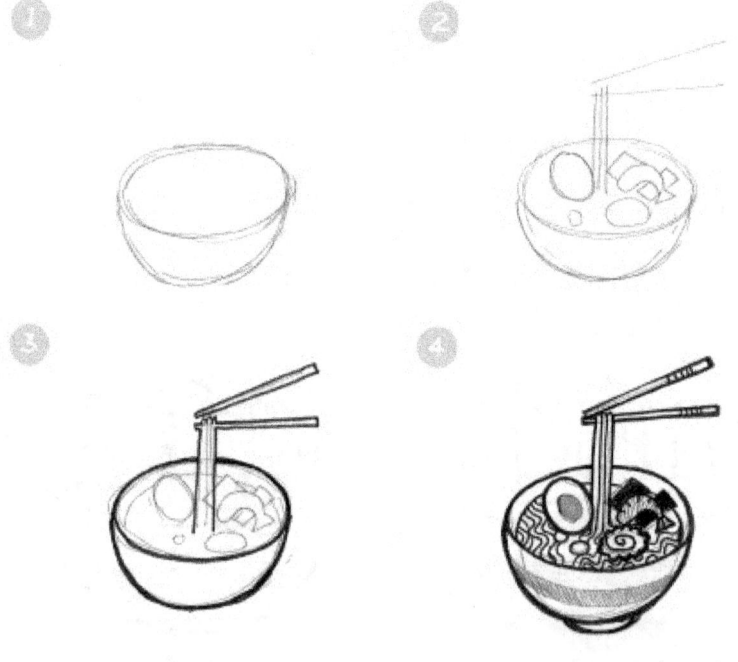

Sushi

We *could* draw our sushi front-on, using one-point perspective, but this is a great opportunity to try some *isometric perspective* instead. With isometric perspective, ovals are still ovals, but any diagonal lines are at roughly 30 degrees. The beauty of drawing this way is that you can draw several objects and no matter where they are located in the picture, they'll look like they all 'belong together' in the same view.

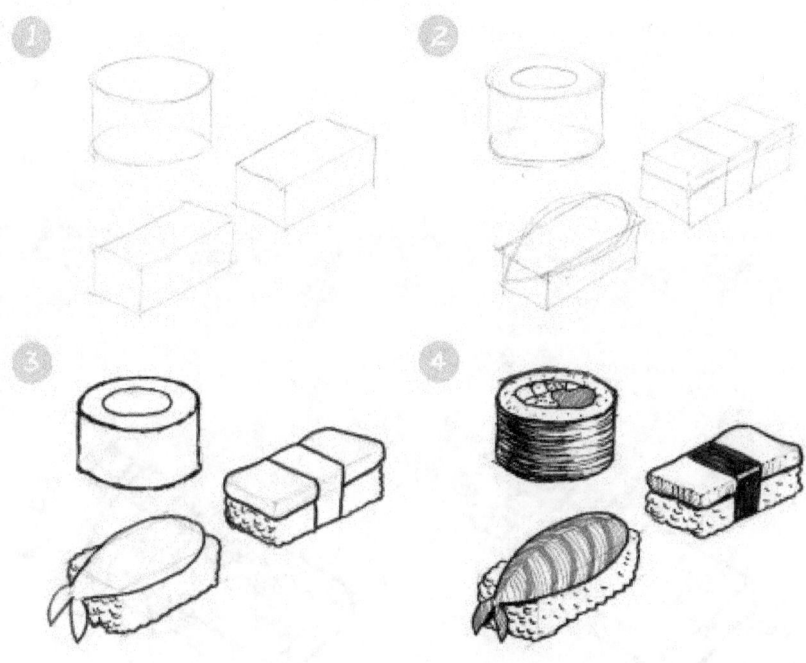

Chocolate bar

What better way to finish off our section on food and drink than with a delicious-looking bar of chocolate?

Start your chocolate bar sketch with the foundation lines of a long shallow box (a bit like you did for the sushi). You can sketch your block all nice and new and ready to eat, or with a big cheeky bite taken out of it, just like I've done. A little bit of shading will help the 'raised squares' effect of the moulded chocolate, too.

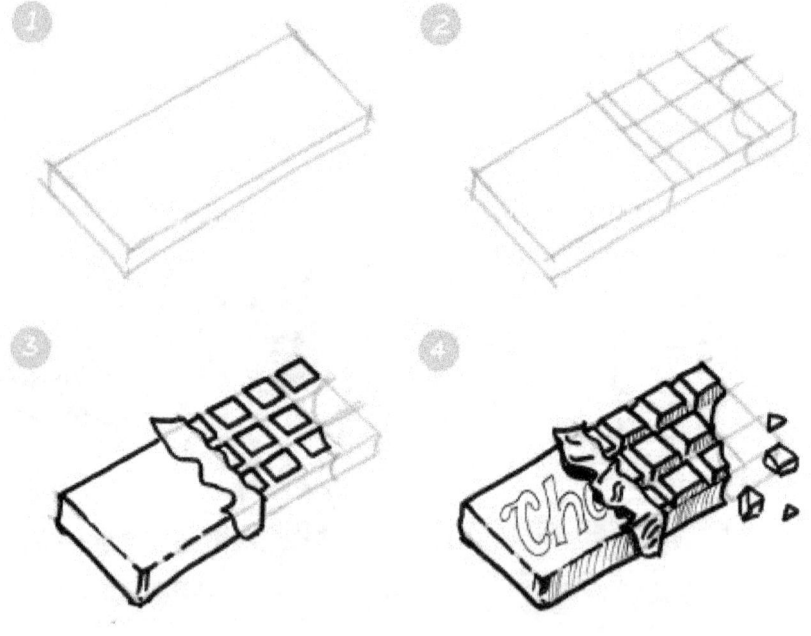

Figures and poses

A simple sketch of a figure can say so much, thanks to the body language we use, and the way we interact with each other.

So as you try these practice sketches, use this as an opportunity to observe the way that people move, stand, react to one another, and so on, and take those observations into your own sketching. I guarantee that if you do that, your sketches will really start to have a life of their own.

What you'll draw in this section

Shrugging, speaking, skeleton, talking in profile, hugging, mask, meditating, sitting with knees up, swinging, leapfrogging, robots, taking a selfie, sitting together, mum and child, and dad and child

Shrugging

The secret to drawing a shrugging figure is to leave a bit of room for the neck. That way, there's some space for the shoulders to tilt upwards a bit, without running into the head.

Tilting the head slightly, and showing hands with palms outward are nice touches for a shrugging figure, too. Oh, and don't forget to put a bit of a confused look on your figure's face!

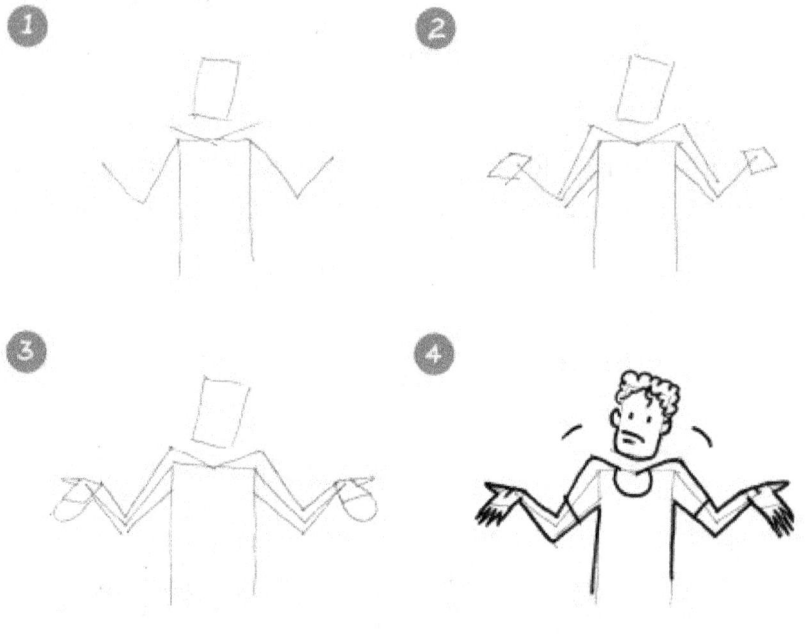

Speaking

Putting a figure behind a podium not only makes them look a lot more important, it means that you don't have to draw their legs!

Once you've done your foundation lines, draw the podium with your black marker first, and then the head, body and hands 'behind' it (3). You can accessorise your podium and figure a bit, depending on what character you'd like the speaker to have, or what conference they're at.

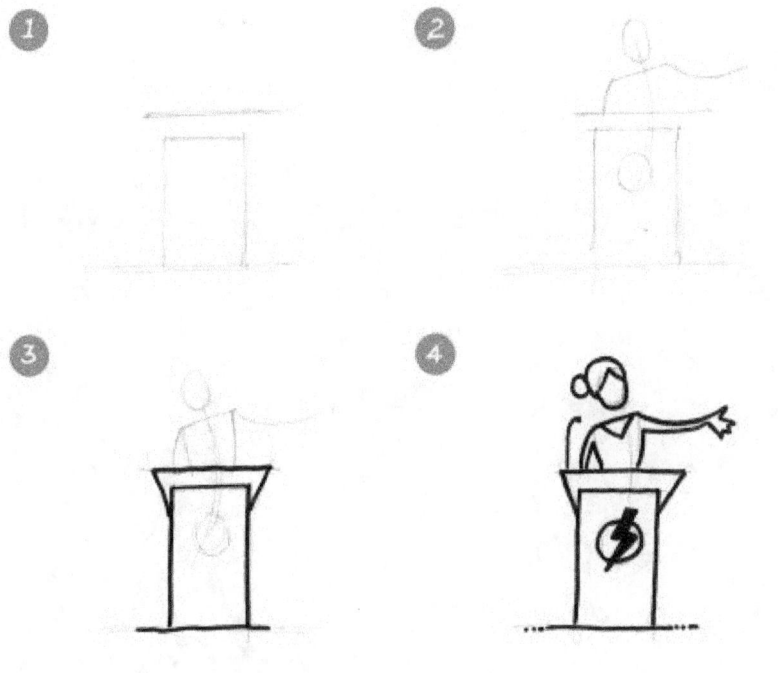

Skeleton

Drawing a skeleton is good practice for drawing the 'architecture' of a figure, plus they just look really cool.

If I know the figure I'm drawing is going to be in a regular standing position, I tend to start with two slightly curved lines for the sides of the body and legs – curved lines are a bit more dynamic than plain straight ones. As with most of these 4-step drawings, a little bit of detail goes a long way.

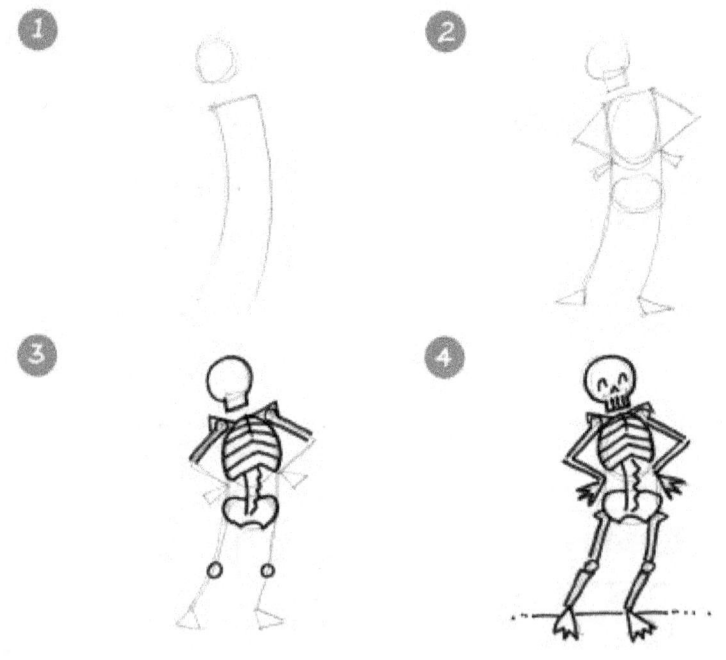

Talking in profile

As we've seen in the figures we've sketched already, we can communicate a lot with body language (shrugging, and so on). But sooner or later, the figures you draw will have to say something, so this is a good time to add a speech balloon.

Including a hand doing something expressive really adds to the story of what's going on in your drawing, too.

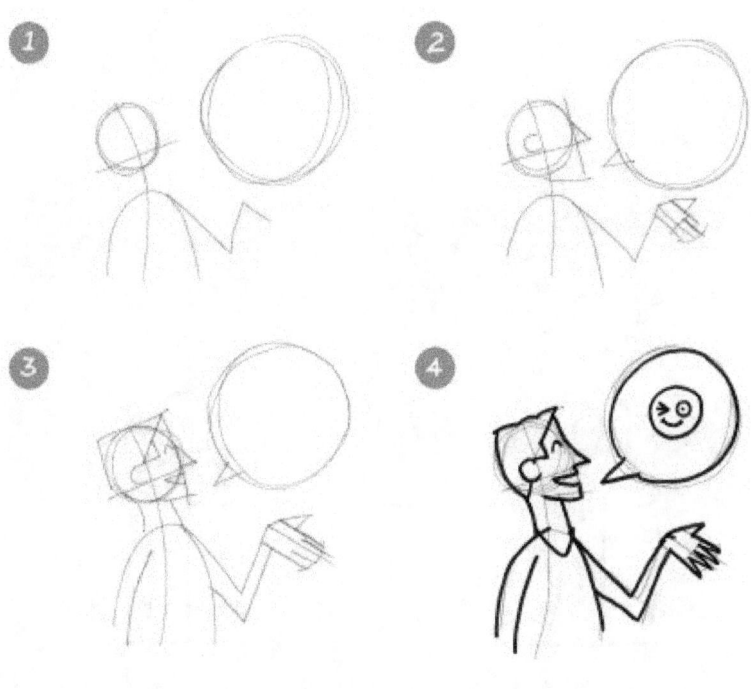

Hugging

Who doesn't love a hug? Trying to draw all those arms going around bodies can be pretty tricky, but here's an easy way to do it.

Starting with a vertical centre foundation line, and lines for the two bodies either side of it is a good base to then sketch tilted heads and arms. Do make sure that the heads overlap only slightly, otherwise it'll look like a *very* awkward hug!

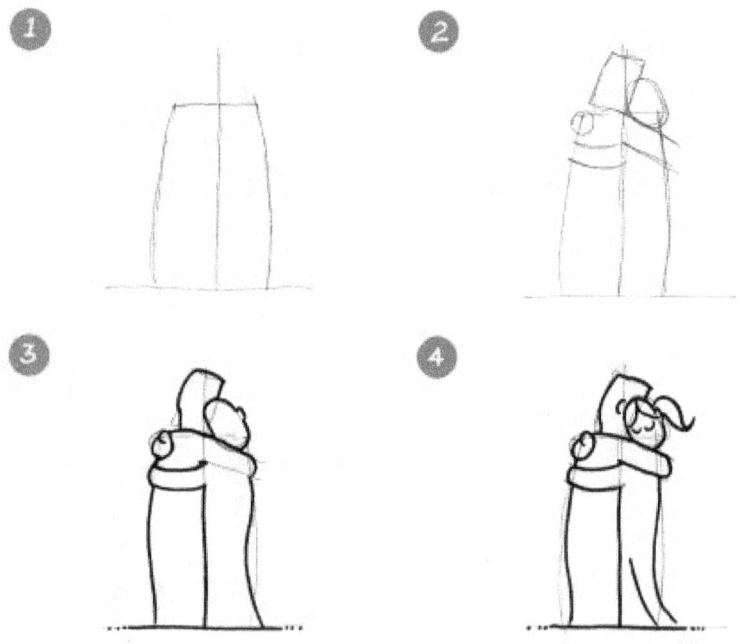

Mask

It's fun to wear masks for dress-ups and times like Halloween. But masks can also be metaphorical: we can hide behind a false smile to hide how we're really feeling, or we can hide behind headphones or dark glasses as a way to ward off unwanted conversation.

Sometimes it can healthy – funny, even – to call out these metaphorical masks by actually drawing them.

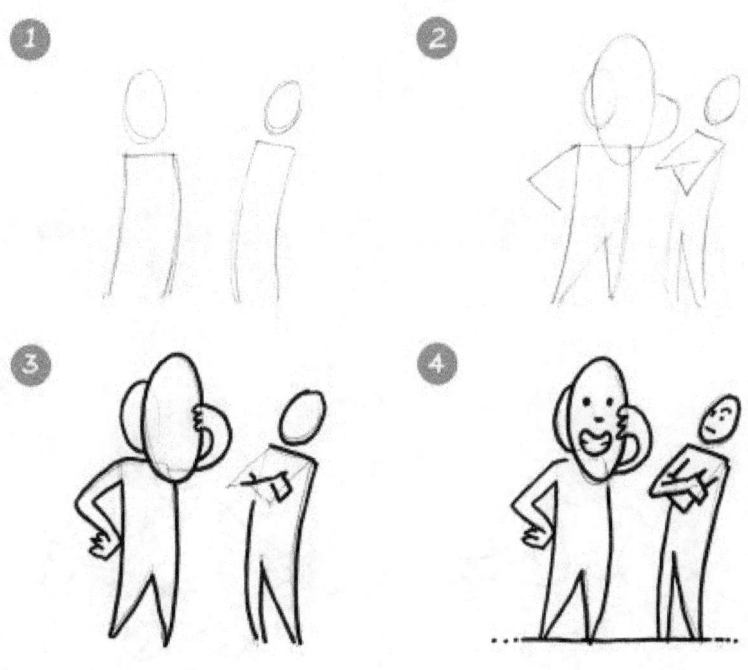

Meditating

This figure is a nice exercise in drawing discipline and precision, and once you get the framework right, it's much easier to flesh it out with details.

In this 4-step drawing, I'm using little circles to visually locate the hands and feet. Sometimes it's nice to add some careful detail to the hands, if it adds meaning to your drawing; I've drawn this meditating figure's hands in the 'Jnana Mudra' position.

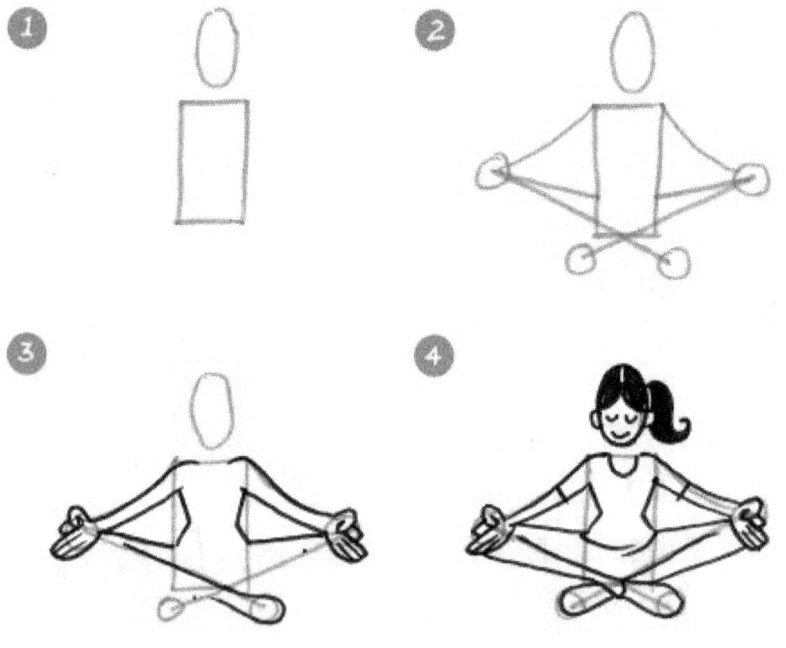

Sitting with knees up

People tend to sit in all sorts of funny and interesting ways, and being able to observe and capture these poses in a sketch can really make your figures come to life.

Notice in this sketch how I've located both hands together as a small circle. This circle becomes two simple 'mitten'-shaped hands placed together. Finish your sketch with some flowing hair or jewellery for interest.

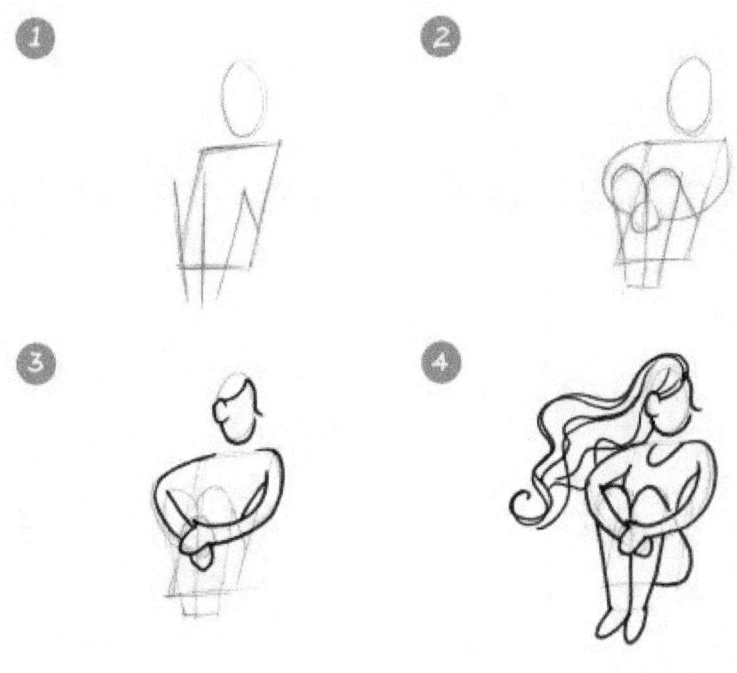

Swinging

This pose is an interesting exercise in sketching a figure at a completely different angle than usual. You can also experiment by exaggerating this pose a bit. You could, for example, sketch the head of your figure being thrown back in delight a lot more than what I've done here.

Notice how I've drawn the hands with a very simple 'holding' pattern here, which you can use in other figures too. Wheeeeee!

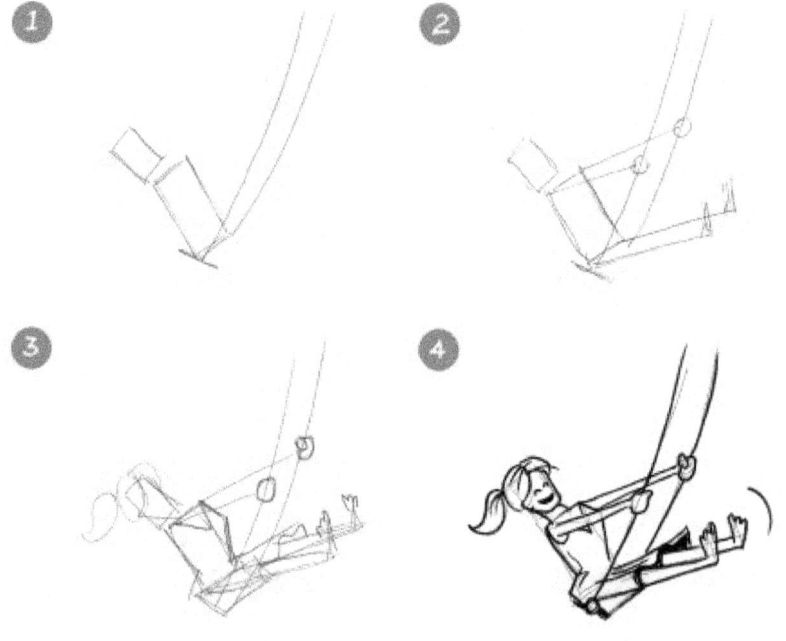

Leapfrogging

While we're sketching figures having fun on swings and so on, let's sketch two leapfrogging figures. This is another great exercise in sketching figures in more visually complex poses.

As you can see, the bottom figure's body is an oval, with the head shape overlapping slightly up and to the left (1). This positioning is important to show the foreshortening and angle of this pose.

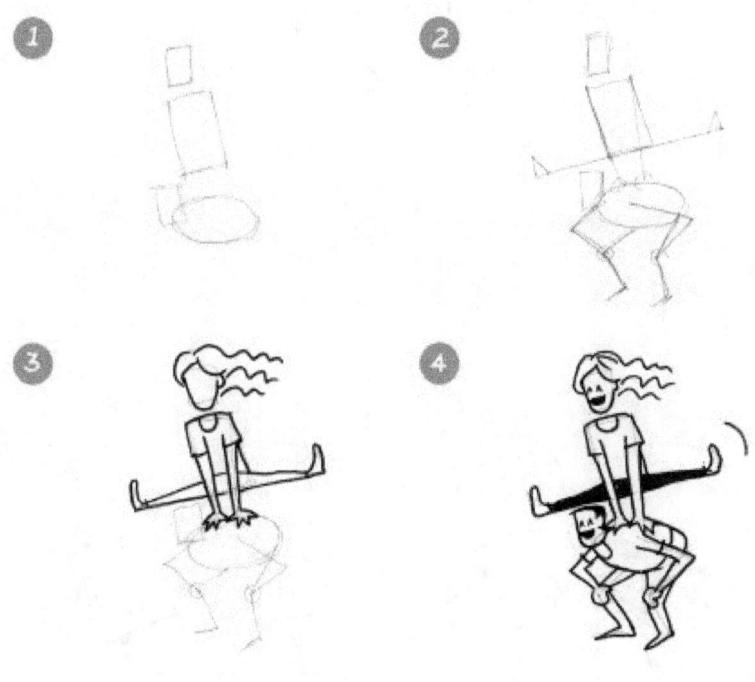

Robots

We love to think of robots as being a lot like us, which is why robots often *look* a lot like us, and *speak* like us. This means that we can sketch robots that look vaguely 'human' (with arms, legs, faces and so on), but we can also get a lot more creative with proportions, in ways that wouldn't work for human figures.

Note how the heads of these figures are much larger by proportion, and how the 'girl' robot doesn't even have legs.

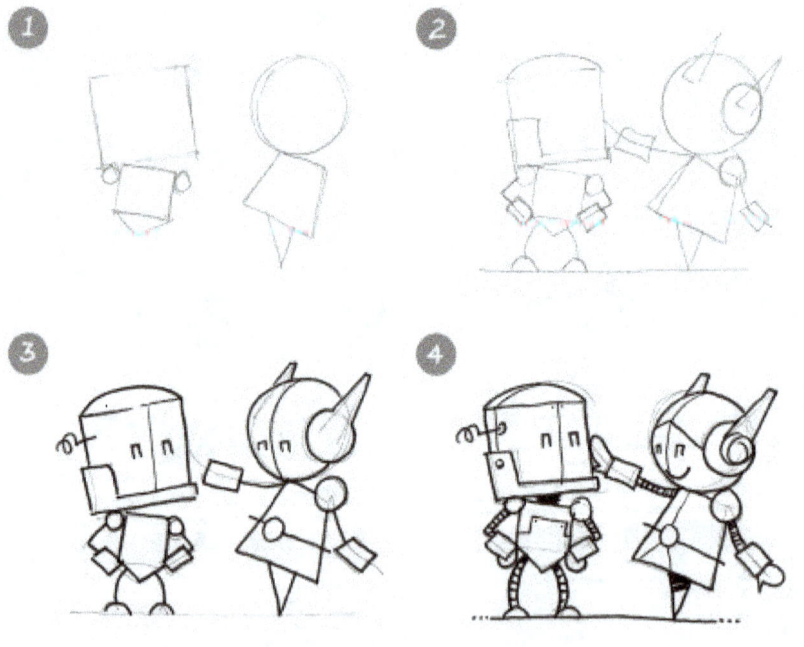

Taking a selfie

Sketching figures is a lot more interesting when you not only have more than figure in the sketch, but also when they're doing fun things together (like leapfrogging, above). Let's try sketching two figures taking a selfie.

Notice how the figures are at an angle to us. You can see this in the mid-lines of the figures, and how the eyes, eyebrows and mouths are drawn slightly to the left in the block of each head.

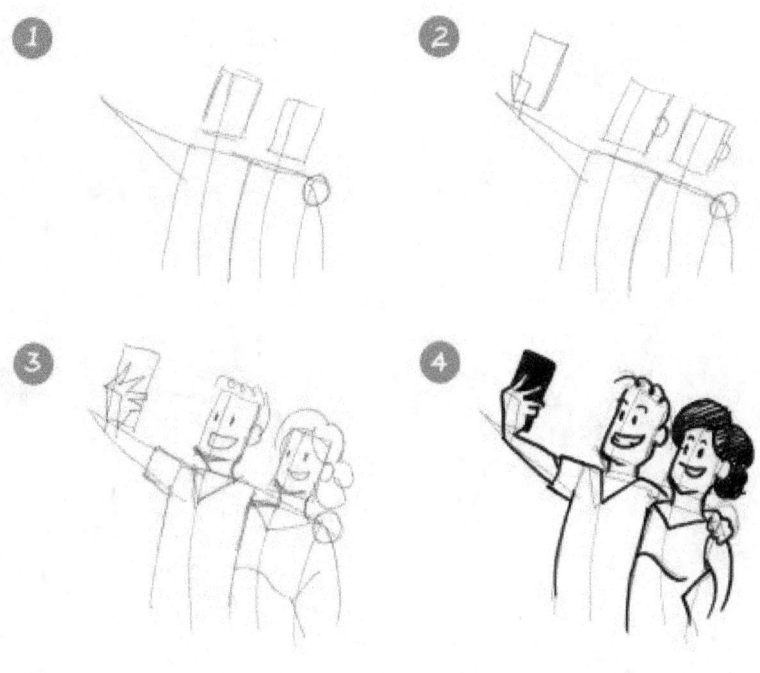

Sitting together

While we're sketching figures doing things together, let's sketch two figures sitting together.

Note the little circle to show where the figures are holding hands (2). If you like, you can extend this sketch to show what the figures are sitting on (like a park bench), and sketch a couple of things to indicate where they are, like some seashells, a beach ball, or a couple of pigeons.

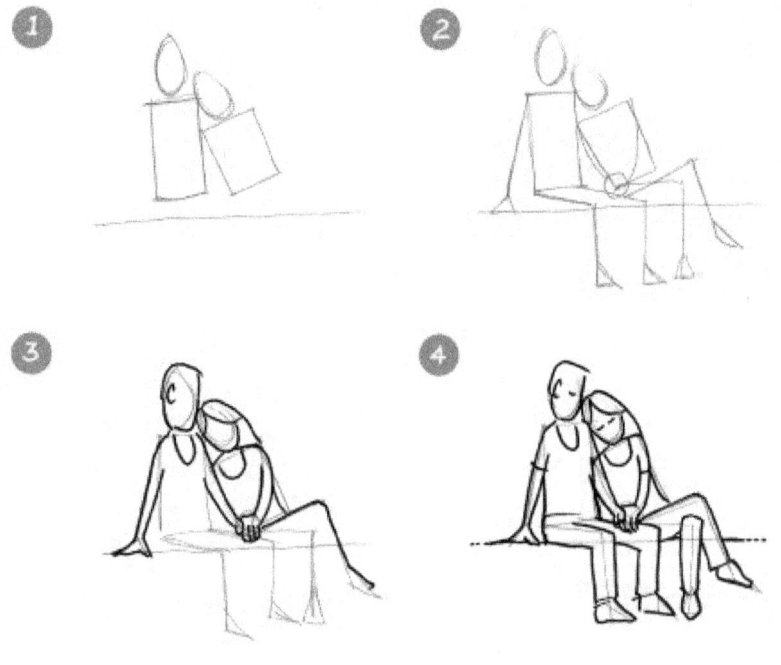

Mum and child

Just like the sketch of two figures hugging, this pose could be quite hard to getting it looking 'right', but breaking down what the arms are doing with foundation lines first makes it much easier.

The positions of the faces are really important for this sketch, so take care with where you place the eyes and mouths, to get that feeling of affection.

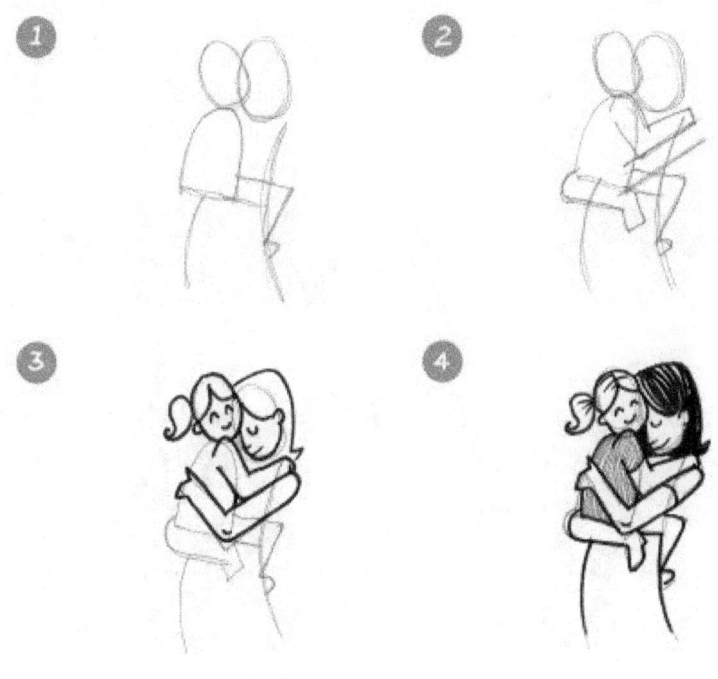

Dad and child

Since we've sketched a mum and child, I thought it'd only be fair to sketch a dad with child as well! Plus, this sketch is another opportunity to show how fun it is seeing figures doing stuff together.

As you ink in your sketch, do the heads first, and then the arms and hands. I like doing the cute little 'stubby starfish' shapes for the child figure (3). Just like the figures taking a selfie, make sure these figures have nice big smiles.

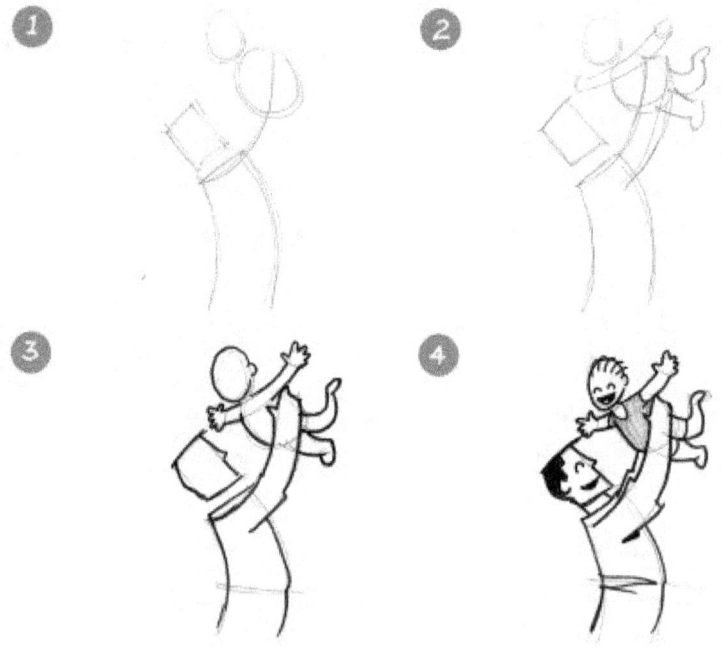

Hands and handling

Just like with figure sketching, hands can show a lot of expression, too. The way we use them to hold things (including other hands) and make signals, can communicate a lot.

Hands are probably the trickiest things to sketch, so remember: go easy on yourself, and practice each pose at least a few times. You can do it!

What you'll draw in this section

Waving, outstretched, pointing, holding a phone, checking the watch, making a fist, rock'n'roll sign, OK sign, presenting, writing, holding a mug, pointing at you, shaking hands, fist bump, and love heart sign.

Waving

Let's start this section by looking at an open hand. This is an opportunity to visually break down the structure of the hand into separate components. 'Seeing' hands in this way will help you to think about how to approach any hand pose you need to draw.

This is your set of basic hand foundation lines. The rest of the sketches we'll do are all about how these components relate to each other.

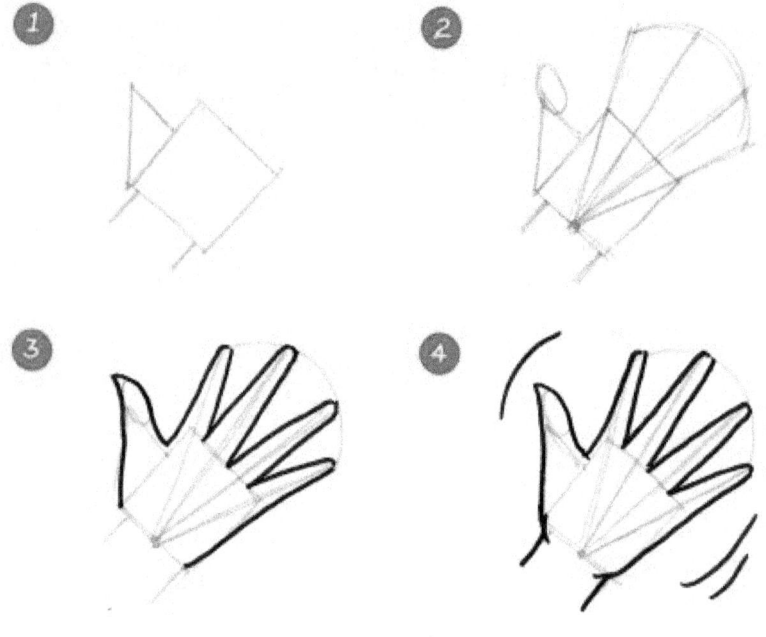

Outstretched

Sometimes we need to draw hands that are viewed on the side, front-on, or in perspective. Let's try two outstretched hands, where they get larger the closer they are to us.

Start with two squares for the palms of the hands, but draw them so that the top sides are narrower than the bottom sides, to show that they are further away from us. Add a line through the middle to help us anchor the fingers, and draw a 'U' shape for each set of fingers (1).

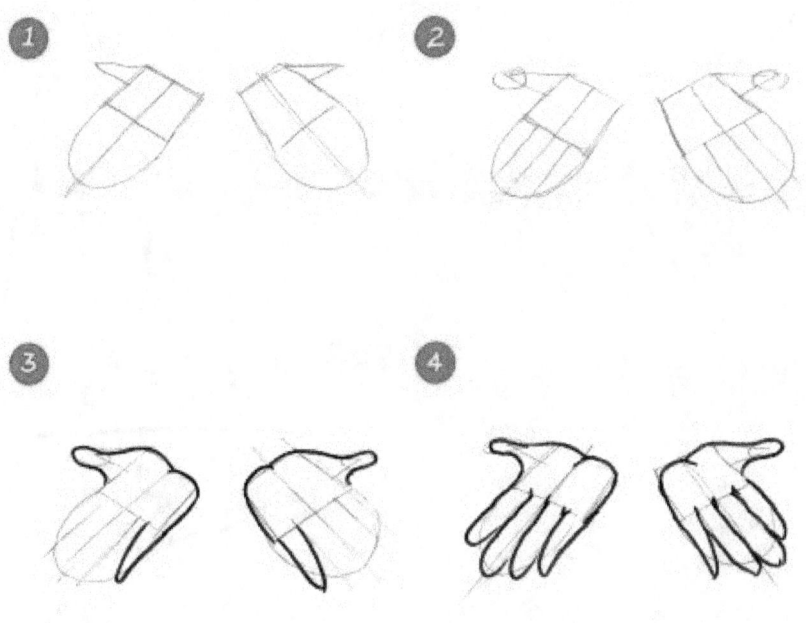

Pointing

If you think of the palm of the hand as a shallow square box, from the side we only see one narrow side of that box, so go ahead and sketch that 'side' as a narrow rectangle.

Extend a line to the right (which will become the forefinger), and sketch a circle to show where the rest of the fingers will curl around underneath (1). As a guide, the length of the forefinger is roughly the same as the length of the 'palm box'.

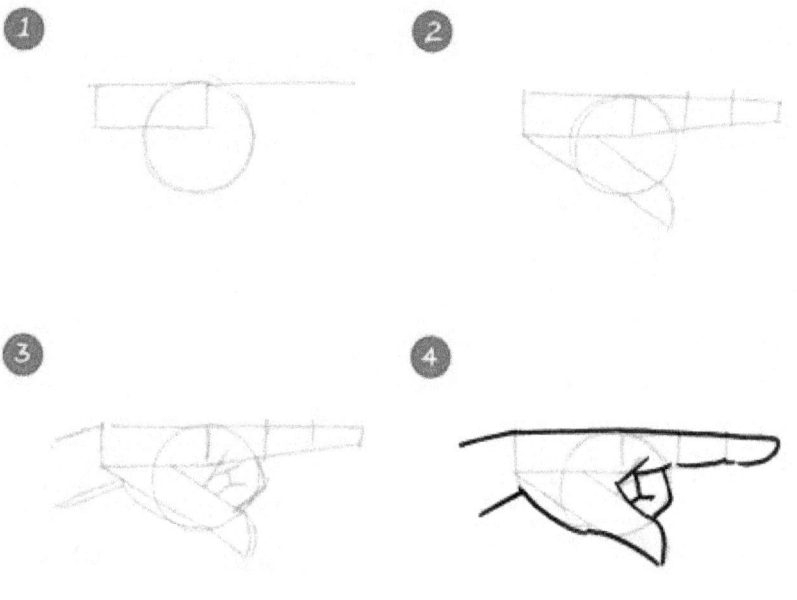

Holding a phone

This sketch is good practice for thinking about – and sketching – how thumbs and fingers curl around objects when we hold them. Sketch the square for the palm at an angle to the rectangle for the phone. *Where* you place that square (and the *proportions*) will drive how well your sketch will 'work' visually, and comes with practice (1). Note the line through the middle of the square, and the 'U' shape, to help you position where the fingers go.

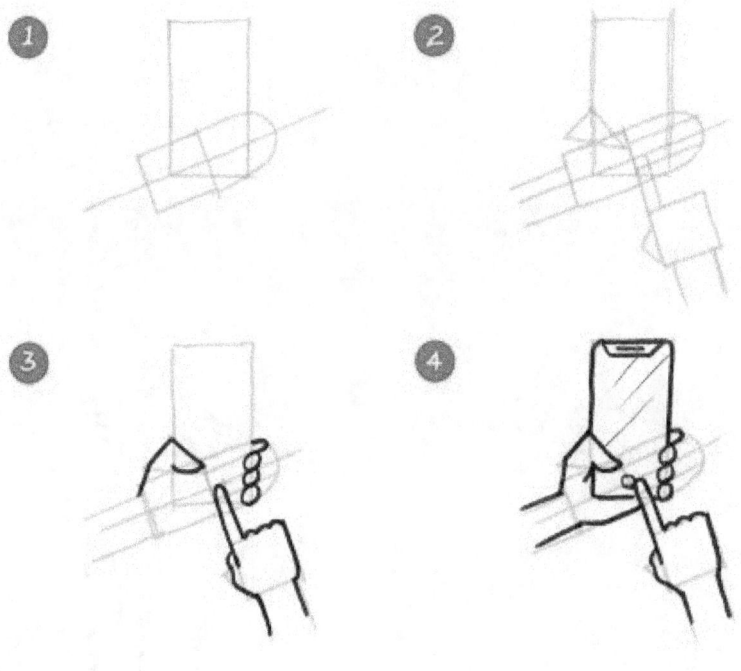

Checking the watch

This sketch gives us practice at viewing how the shape of the thumb changes as the hand rotates, as well as sketching a pointing hand from above again.

Note how the fingers of the left hand curl underneath, with each finger gradually curling a little more. Finish off your sketch by going around the outside with the black marker first, and then going back over it to mark in the shapes of fingers and thumbs.

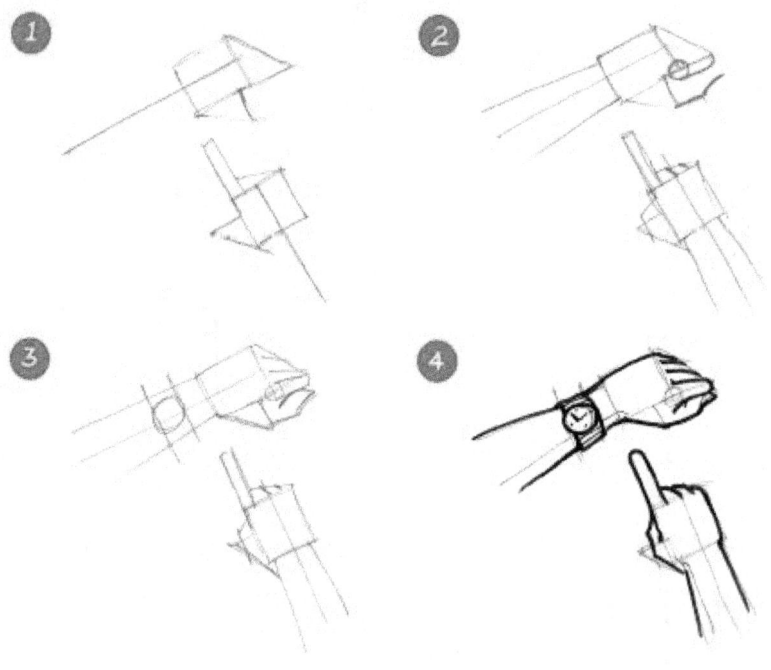

Making a fist

Just to prepare you: sketching a fist is really tricky. Stick with it, and you'll soon 'click' as to how you can make each component – the palm, the thumb, and the fingers, visually 'work' together.

Remember, it's also easier to go around the outside in black marker first (once you've done the foundation lines), and then draw in the details of the thumb locked over the fingers.

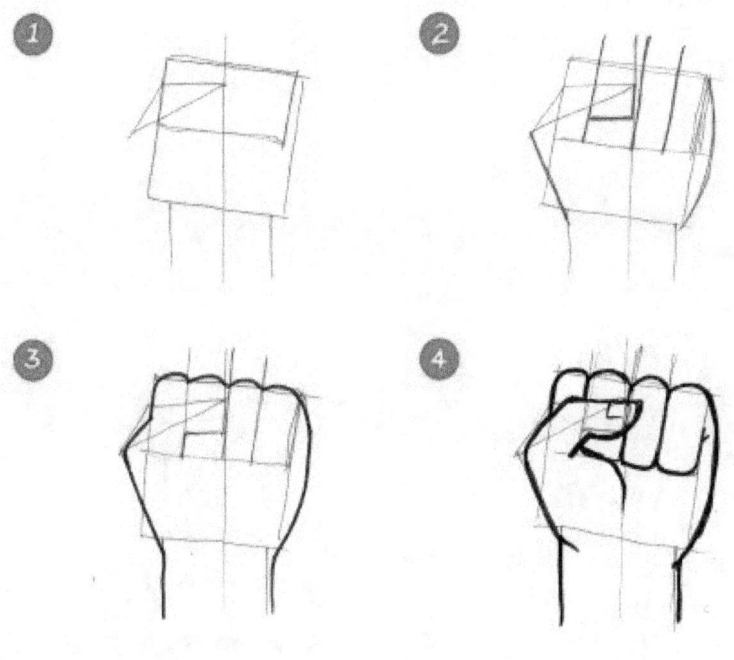

Rock'n'roll sign

This 'rock'n'roll' sign is fun to sketch, plus it's good practice thinking about – and showing—how the fingers and thumb work together. Careful using this hand sign in Spain, Greece and Italy, though: in those countries, it's called the 'corna', where it's made towards a man to imply that his wife is cheating on him. Yikes!

As with all of these hand sketches, practice pays off. Don't forget to accessorise that hand. Rock on!

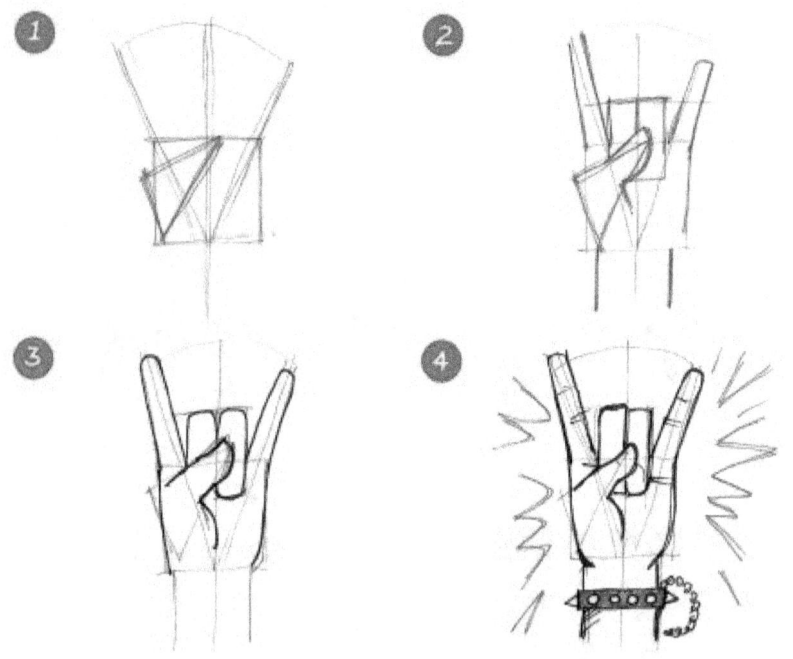

OK sign

Just like the 'rock'n'roll' sign, you have to be careful where you use this one: apparently in Greece, Spain and Brazil, doing this at someone doesn't mean 'OK' at all, it's actually quite offensive.

As you draw around the outside in black marker, think about how each finger is partly hiding behind the one in front of it. Oh, and of course you can always use your own hand as a model to help you!

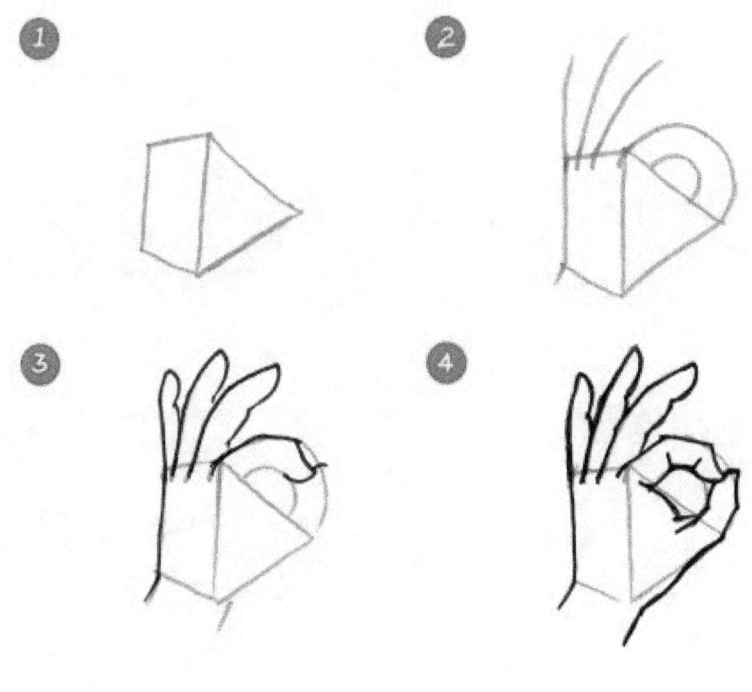

Presenting

This hand pose is a neat way to show something being presented or supported.

We don't see much of the 'shallow square box' of the palm in this pose, so start with a broad triangle instead (1). This is a great example of how foundation lines can really drive the success of the final drawing, with that larger oval on the left side of the triangle, and the smaller oval for the end of the thumb as well.

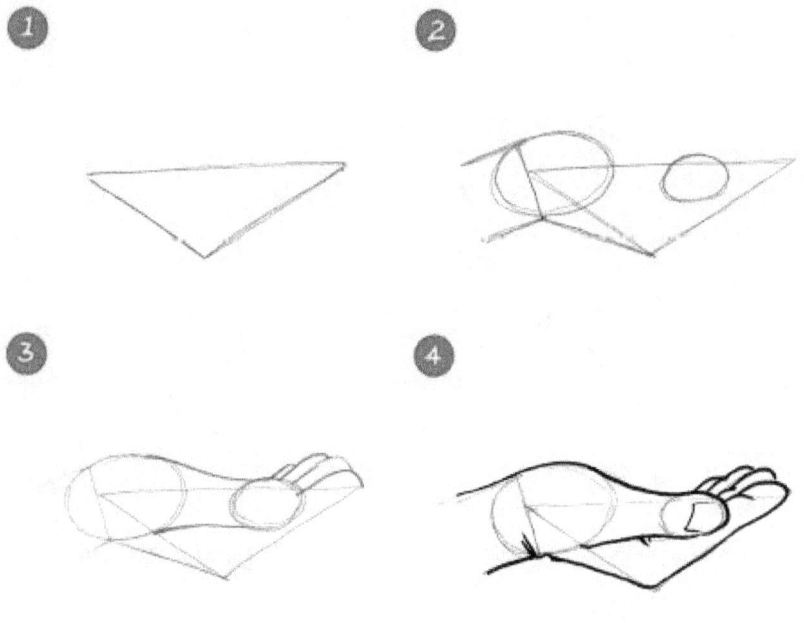

Writing

This is another hand pose that uses a big triangle as a base. Sketch a long diagonal as a guideline for the pencil, and then use this to help you locate two small circles for the first knuckle of the forefinger and the first joint of the thumb.

Don't forget to show the tips of the other fingers peeking underneath from behind the thumb, too.

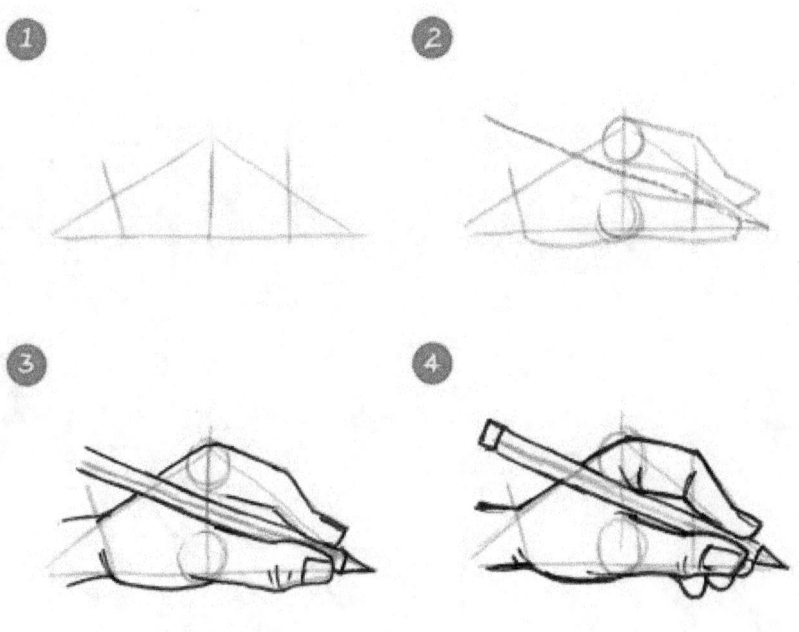

Holding a mug

Sometimes when the hand is holding things of various shapes and sizes, its shape seems to change altogether, making it even harder to draw than usual. Often it's easier to draw the object being held *first*, so go ahead and sketch the mug (1).

Now, sketch a rhomboid shape for the palm, two parallel lines to show where the thumb will go, and a couple of ovals to show the fleshy parts of the palm.

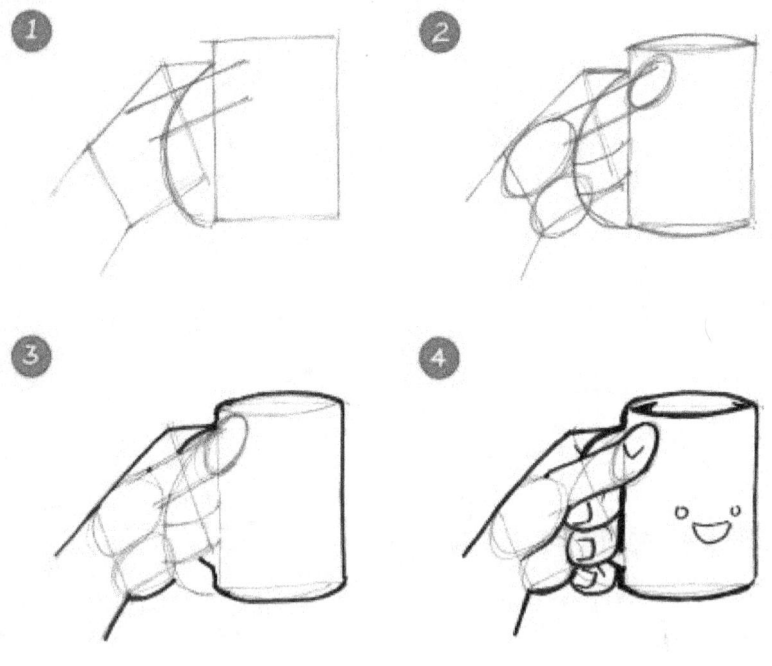

Pointing at you

I won't lie: this pose is probably one of the trickiest to draw. That said, it's made easier with a foundation line of a nice big circle (with vertical and horizontal middle lines) and then a small circle in the top left 'quadrant' (1) that becomes the forefinger coming out at you.

The fingernail and thumbnail give us visual 'cues' about how the thumb and forefinger are positioned, and help it to look 'right'.

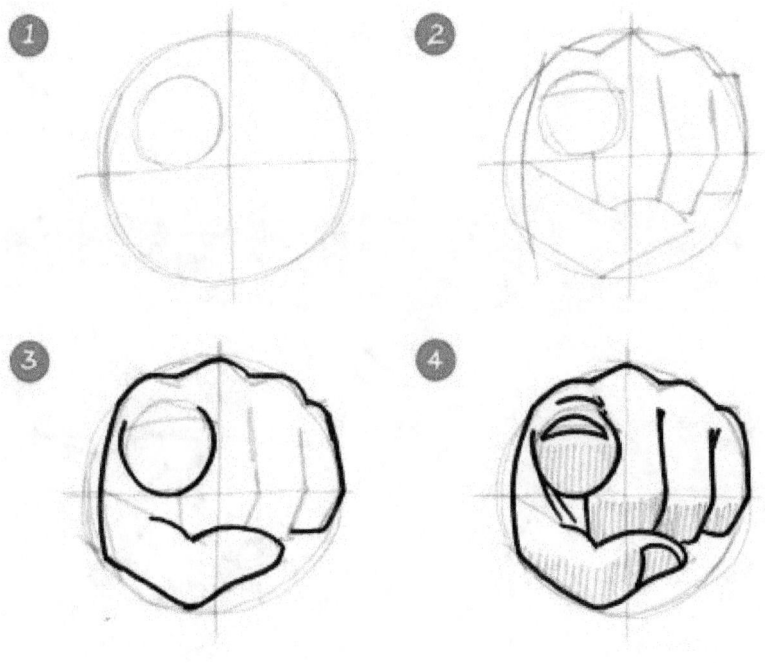

Shaking hands

You can actually sketch this pose based on one oval, but sketching it that way *first* robs you of 'seeing' and understanding what the wrist, thumb and finger components of each hand are doing as the wrap around each other.

Finishing off the foreshortened fingers popping out from underneath as little circles is a nice touch.

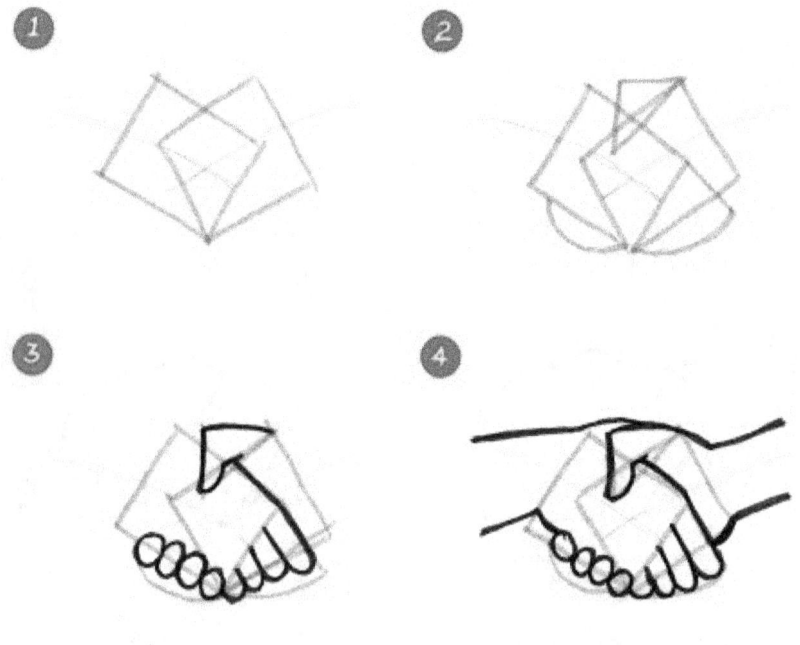

Fist bump

This sketch starts out looking a bit like an insect's face, but trust me, it's all about helping to position the thumbs and fingers in the right way!

As you go around the outside with your black marker, you'll see the fist shapes coming together. The curves of the thumb and the little 'I' shapes that show the curled fingers make all the difference in this one.

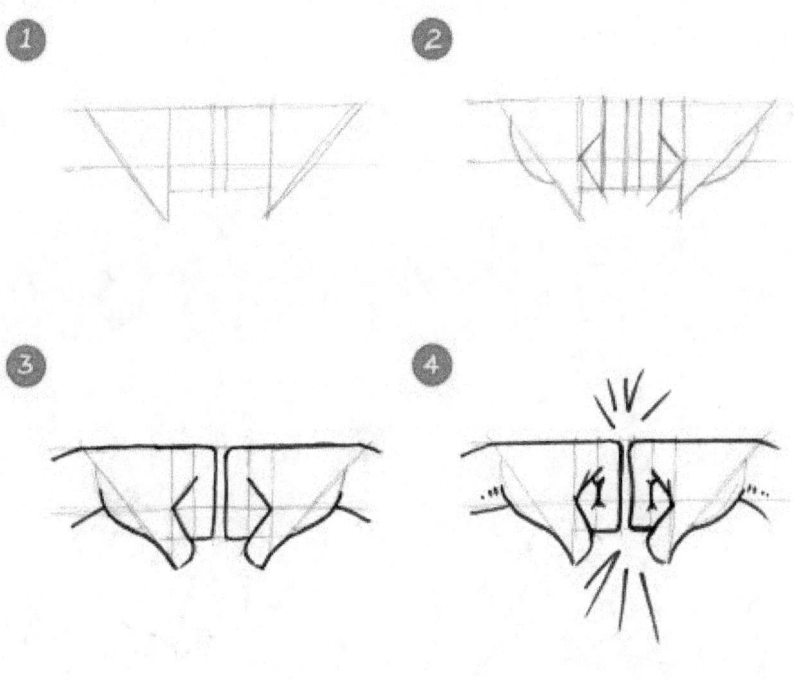

Love heart sign

We'll finish off this section on a positive note: a love heart sign! Just like the fist bump sketch, this one starts off in a funny way, but it's only to help you get the lines in the right place from the start.

Remember from the pointing hand sketch how fingers are curved on the bottom, and straight on top? Do that again, as you draw in the fingers in this sketch, as well as how each finger peeks out from behind the one in front of it.

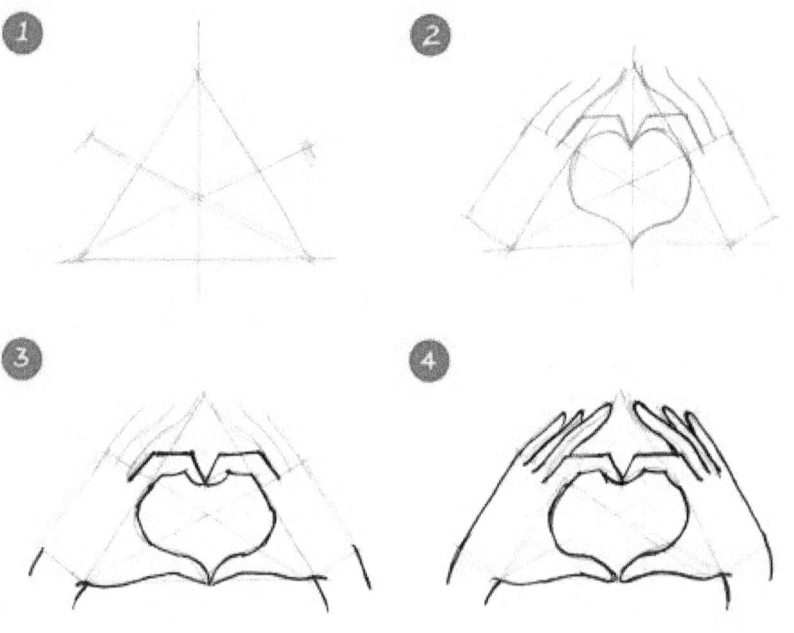

Pop culture and symbols

This section is dedicated to the artists and artisans, the musicians and movie-makers, the icons and symbols of our time and times past.

Many of these objects work really well as visual metaphors, and come in handy for storytelling, and activating people's imaginations. Hopefully sketching these objects prompts you to think of your own favourite things to sketch from popular culture.

What you'll draw in this section

Sugar skull, cogs, coffee pot, electric guitar, crown, megaphone, genie lamp, trophy, arcade game, treasure chest, Converse sneaker, gas mask, jack-in-the-box, money, and a Stormtrooper.

Sugar skull

Sugar skulls (or *calaveras de azucar*) are used to decorate gravestones and altars during the Day of Dead (*Dia de los Muertos*), to remember loved ones who've passed away. They're also incredibly popular as face make-up, tattoos, and decorations on clothing and jewellery.

You can go nuts with decorating and colouring in your sugar skull sketch. Be sure to decorate the eyes with flowers; flowers symbolise life!

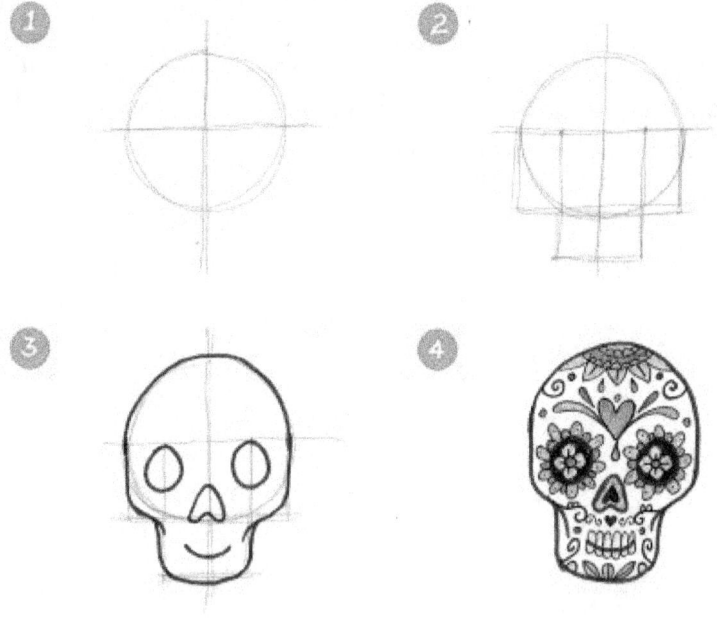

Cogs

Cogs and gears are a great metaphor to represent systems, machines, settings... anything technical, really. This sketch is also a great exercise in precision and patience.

An easy way to sketch this one is to start with one circle first, and use your foundation lines to break it into quarters, and then eighths (1). You can ink in the cogs at the end if you like (4), or leave them 'open'; it's up to you.

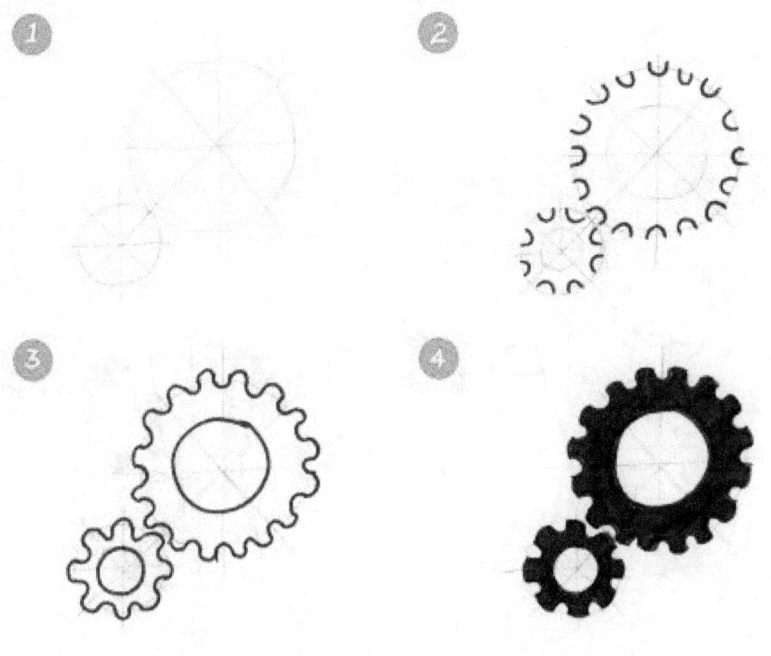

Coffee pot

I still remember the first time I bought a Bialetti coffee pot (or *Moka pot*, named after the Yemenite city of Mocha). An Italian engineer named Alfonso Bialetti patented this design back in 1933, and this icon of industrial art is still very much in use today.

Finish it off with a few details, and make sure you ink in the handle and the top knob, which helps to make this coffee pot design so distinctive!

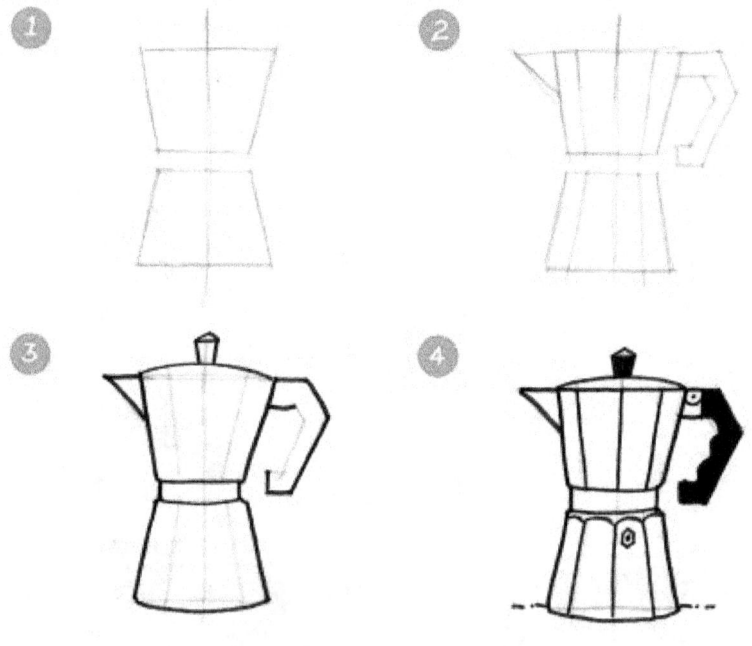

Electric guitar

If you're not already a rock star, then you'll definitely be one once you can smash out a picture of an electric guitar whenever you want to.

Use the foundation line blocks as a guide to ink in some cool sweeping lines for the guitar body. Add in some details, like the pickups and volume dials, and you're done!

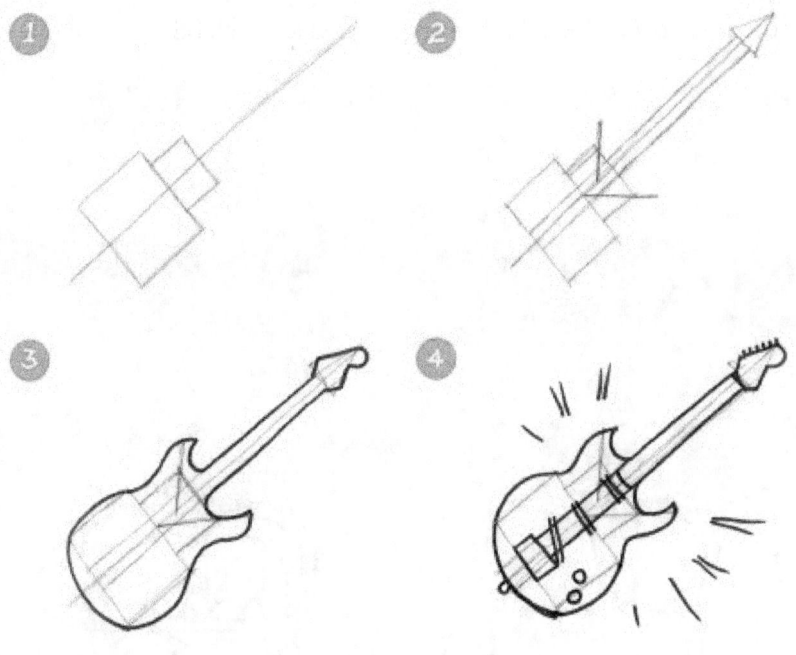

Crown

Crowns come in all shapes and sizes, from little tiaras to massive cake-of-diamonds Crown of Queen Elizabeth II. The one I've drawn here is actually called a hoop crown.

As you can see, it's totally okay if your foundation lines are messy; that's the great thing about foundation lines! Use the circles as guides to add the 'half arches' that go from the *circlet* (base), to the *monde* at the top of the crown. Finish it all off with gems and as much bling as you like.

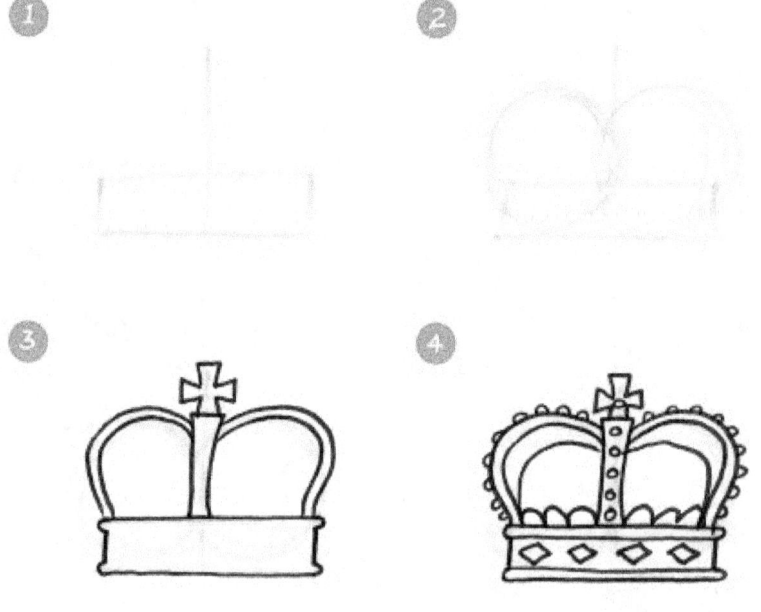

Megaphone

We can thank the ancient Greeks for what we know today as the megaphone, when they used conical devices to project their voices in theatre and the senate. Believe it or not, it was actually Thomas Edison who invented the megaphone in 1878, and named it 'megaphone' from the Greek words *megas* ('great') and *phone* ('voice').

Don't forget to add some flashy lines out the front, to show how LOUD your megaphone is!

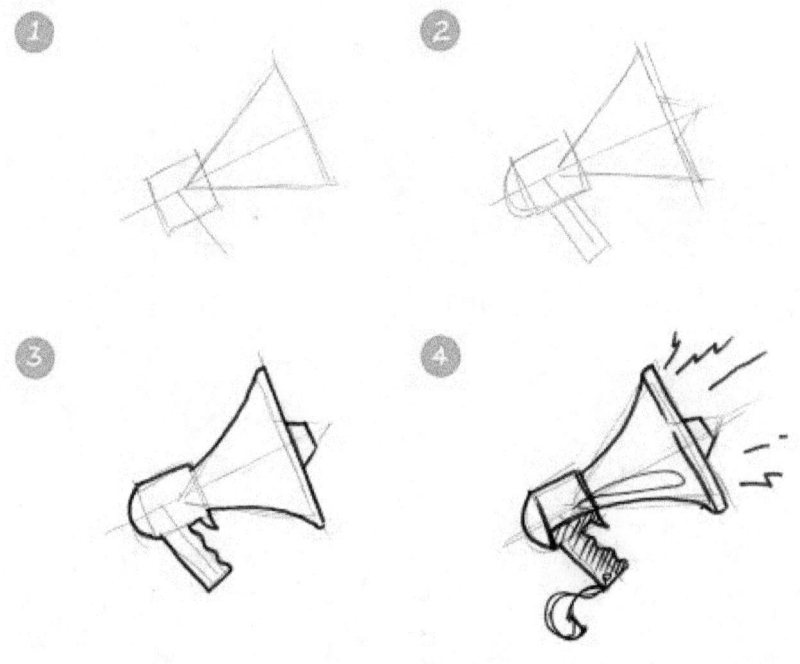

Genie lamp

Thanks to the legendary tales in *Arabian Nights*, these oil lamps evoke images of genies and flying carpets in magical faraway lands. Genies (also called *jinn* in Arabic) are spirits in ancient Middle Eastern and African cultures. The thing about genies popping out of oil-burning lamps like these comes from Islam-associated mythology, where a *jinni* could be controlled by magically binding it to any ordinary household object, like a lamp.

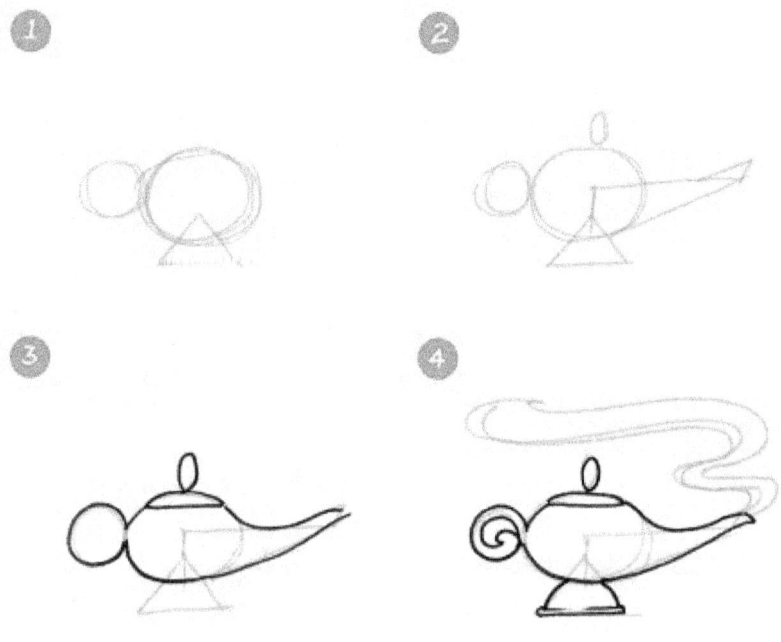

Trophy

Start your trophy sketch with a long vertical line (1); that helps you keep everything as symmetrical as possible.

Add a square and small rectangle for the body of the trophy, and a long triangle for the neck and base. Add a couple of circles on the side to guide where the handles will go (2). Once you get the hang of these main elements – the head, neck and handles – you can go nuts and make them any shape and size you like. Winner!

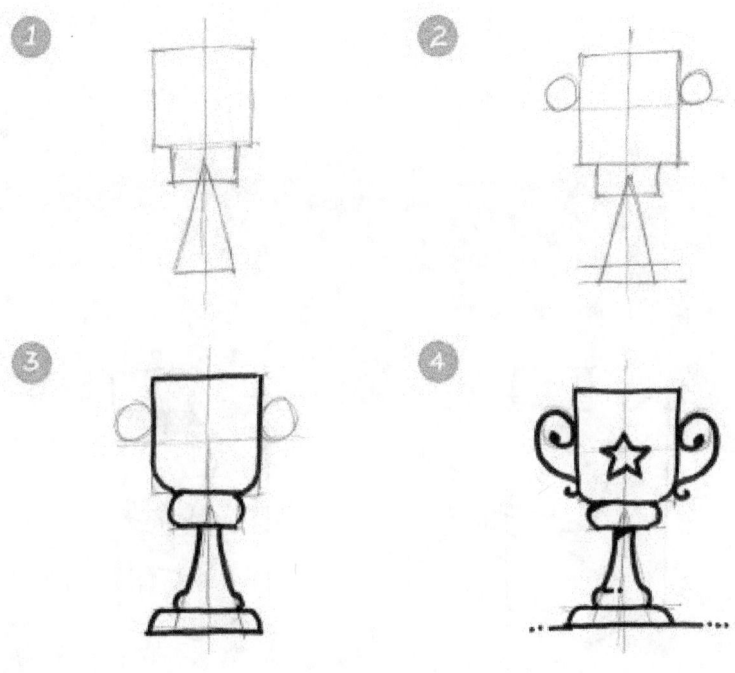

Arcade game

I don't want to even *think* about the amount of cash I must have put into machines like this when I was a kid, but I still had a massive amount of fun on them, that's for sure.

Sketching an arcade game in 3D (actually, 2-point perspective) like this, rather than front-on (1-point perspective) accentuates its unique shape. Finish it off with details like the joysticks and coin box covers at the bottom. I feel like playing Donkey Kong right now!

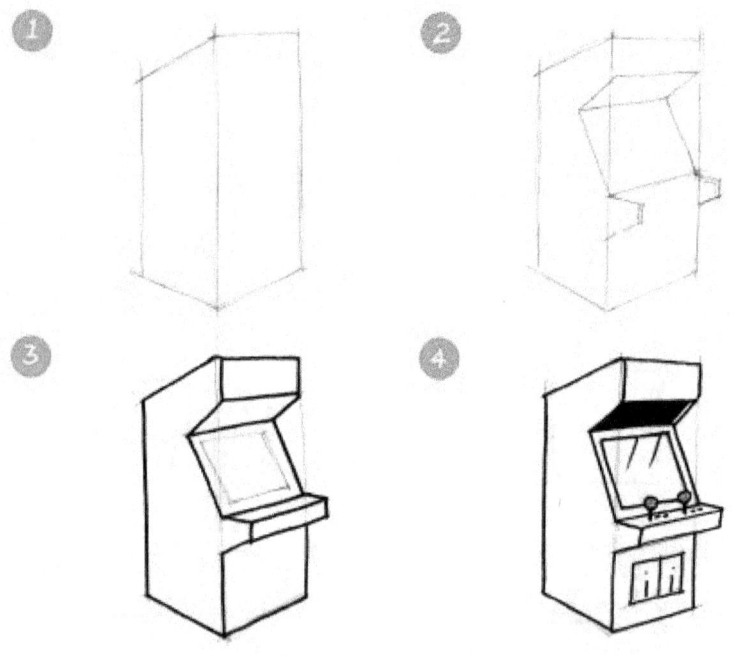

Treasure chest

Treasure chests are a great metaphor for *hidden value*. Despite what we might assume, pirates rarely buried their treasure. History records one dude called William Kidd, who buried some loot on Long Island before sailing into New York City. The *idea* of buried treasure, though, caught on from Robert Louis Stevenson's *Treasure Island* book.

Be sure to dress your treasure chest a few details, and add some coins to show that there be treasure in thar!

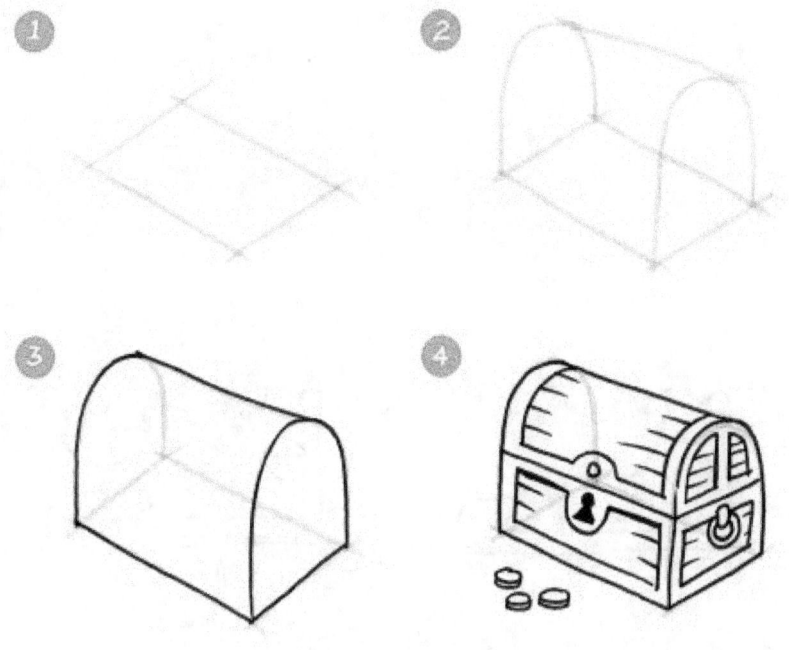

Converse sneaker

As far as iconic footwear goes, it's hard to go past the legendary Chucks. They were first created in 1917, but the design we know and love today was mostly due to Chuck Taylor, an American basketball player and shoe salesman. He joined Converse, and helped them improve the design in 1922.

The foundation lines of the triangle and two rectangles help you start your sketch off with the right proportion.

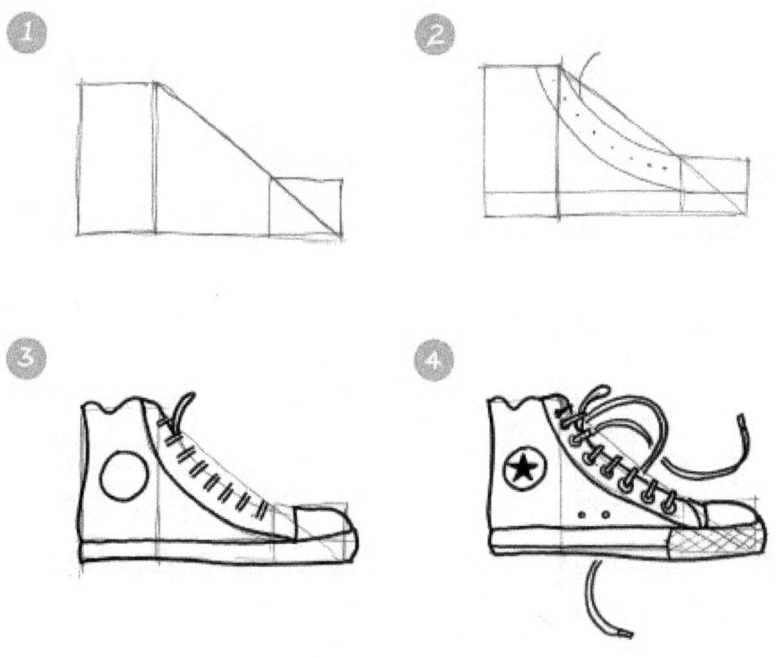

Gas mask

This gas mask sketch is another example where a little bit of care, precision, and detail pay off really well. As before, having a vertical foundation line down the centre helps to keep everything reasonably symmetrical and in place. The two 'eye' circles become pentagon shapes, and the little ovals on either side become filter canisters.

Dress up your drawing with a few 'radiation' signs, and you're ready for whatever apocalypse comes at you!

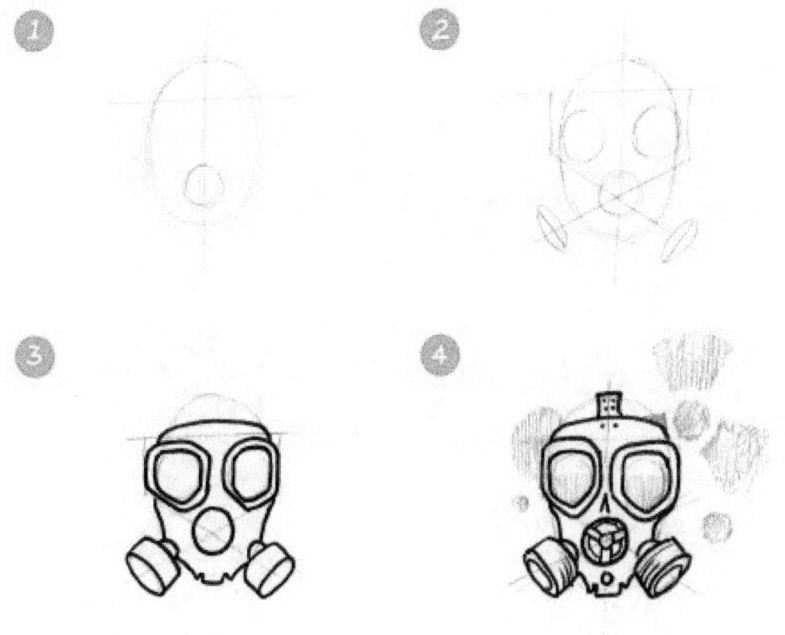

Jack-in-the-box

The jack-in-the-box is a great metaphor for *fun and surprise*. It's usually a little clown that pops out of it, but you can always replace a clown with something else, to make the metaphor more meaningful for you.

Here's a tip: draw in the body, hands and head of your 'jack', and then the lines of the box that are 'behind' it. That way, you don't have to worry about making any lines go 'in front of' the jack by mistake (3).

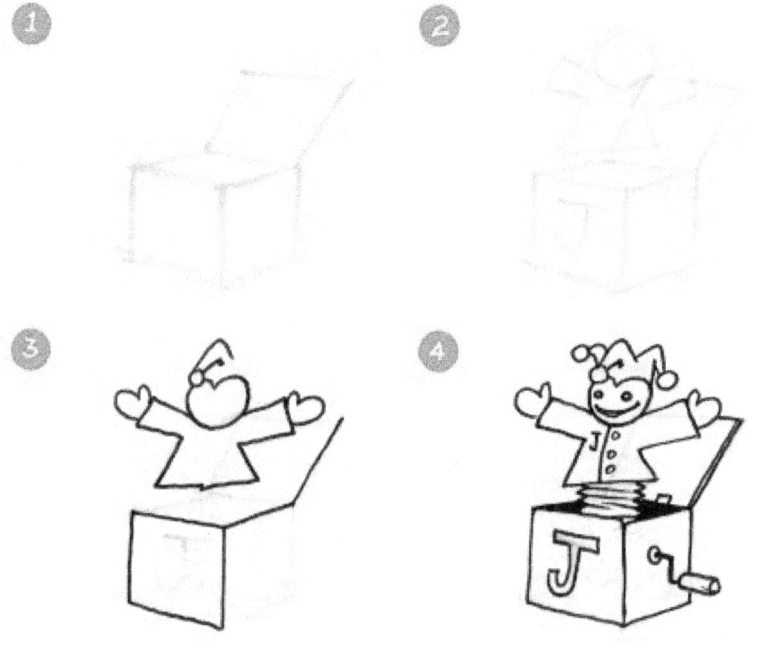

Money

Start your stack of cash (at least a sketch of one, anyway!) with a rough parallelogram or rhomboid shape (1). Sketch two lines underneath that first shape, keeping the lines parallel; this will become the base of the stack of money (2). Add some lines from the edges just to indicate texture, and the idea of many dollar notes (3).

You can always add a few ovals for coins, and a hint of detail on the top note to indicate a face and denomination.

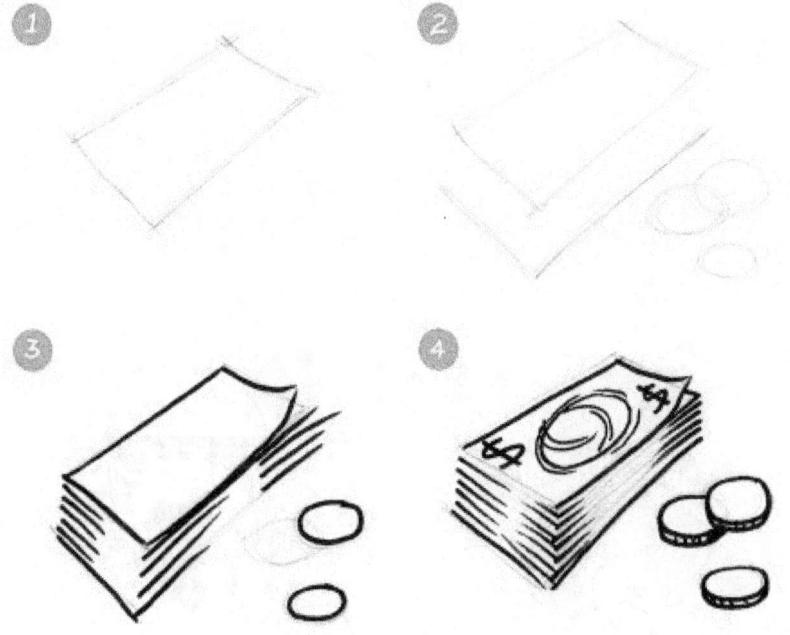

Stormtrooper

Star Wars is such a big part of Western popular culture, and sometimes it seems that the Empire Stormtrooper helmet is everywhere you look: on posters, t-shirts, Instagram.. even in tattoos!

Brace yourself, as this one's pretty complex, but careful foundation lines will reward you with a really cool-looking Stormtrooper helmet. Go around the outside in black marker (3) and start to fill in the details as shown.

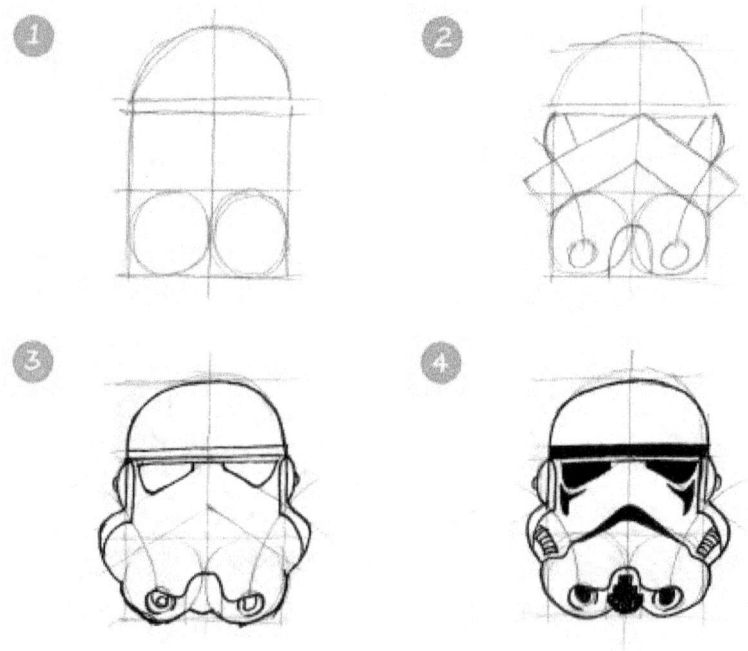

What next?

Now that you've worked your way through over 100 practice sketches, I hope you can see a big improvement in your drawing confidence and capability. Give yourself a well-earned pat on the back!

Here are a few ideas to keep your sketching journey going...

Where will you use your drawings?

As I mentioned at the beginning of this book, **Draw in 4!** is a visual phrase book, to help you add more and more 'words' to your vocabulary, when it comes to visual language and visual expression.

Now it's time to use that visual language, and let all those drawings loose into the world! There are lots of ways you can do that. Here are just a few:

Home art

Is there a particular drawing you did that you really like? You'll be amazed at how great it will look framed! Mount that sketch in a frame (just a cheap frame from a homewares store is perfectly fine), hang it on your wall, and get ready for lots of compliments from everyone who visits.

Greeting cards

Draw your own greeting cards, scan them into your computer, and then get them printed and sent using a service like touchnote.com[1]. It's fun, and so much more lively and personal than a store-bought card.

Sketchnoting

---

1. https://www.touchnote.com/

Try taking notes about what you learn and experience, using pictures as well as words.

You can start with easier things (such as the main points that struck you about a book you've read, or some tips you've picked up from cooking a new type of cuisine), to more advanced things like sketchnoting in real time as you listen to a favourite podcast, a talk at a conference. You can also use sketchnoting as a way of journaling about travels you go on, places you see and people you meet.

It's loads of fun, easy to start, and helps you memorise more and recall more information. Check out sketchnotearmy.com[2] for lots of examples and advice.

Urban sketching

Step outside and sketch what you see around you; the skyline, a building, someone sitting on a park bench, anything! Get inspired by checking out urbansketchers.org[3], and try it yourself.

Visual presentations

Ditch the clip art and bland stock photos, and use your own drawings in your business presentations instead.

It can be daunting at first, but try something simple, like peppering your presentation with basic icons for regular concepts (like *idea*, *goal*, *problem* or *plan*). Once you get more confident with putting these sorts of sketches you're your presentations, you can try for more advanced graphics, where you capture a customer experience problem, or a business plan as a large picture rather than using lots of text. You'll be surprised by the extra engagement you get!

---

2. http://sketchnotearmy.com/

3. http://www.urbansketchers.org/

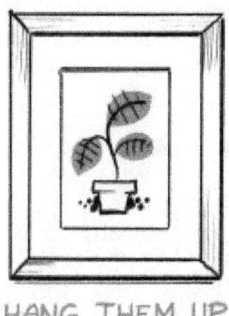

HANG THEM UP

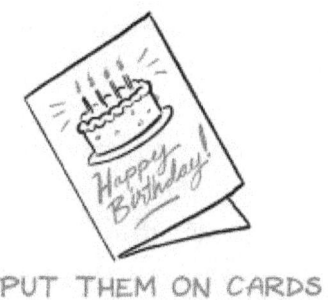

PUT THEM ON CARDS

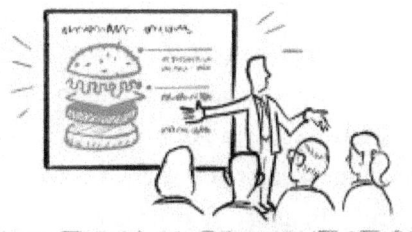

USE THEM IN PRESENTATIONS

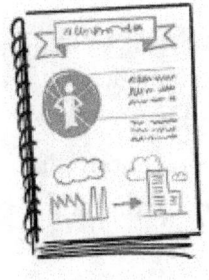

USE THEM IN
SKETCHNOTING

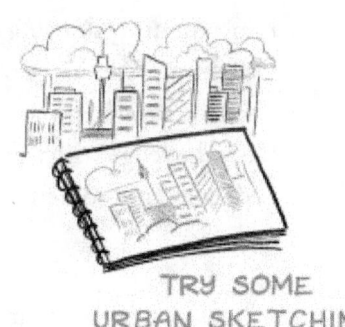

TRY SOME
URBAN SKETCHING

Set yourself challenges

Now that you've worked your way through all these practise sketches
in **Draw in 4!**, you might be up for some other sketching challenges, to
keep your ability and confidence growing in an intentional way.

And the best person to give you these challenges is yourself. It's fun
to stretch yourself with all sorts of challenges, and whatever they are,

it'll be super satisfying to achieve them. Here are some ideas to get you going.

- Get a consistent sketching habit going, like sketching on your work commute every day for two weeks
- Commit to using sketching in a new area of your work (or maybe for the first time at work!), like in your presentations, or live during a meeting
- Draw a 10x10 grid, and fill each square with icons that you might use at work (e.g. document, filter, apple, car, building) and then scan them, slice them up and use them in your presentations instead of boring free stock icons
- Share your sketches on social media; you'll be surprised at how encouraging everyone is when you share your own work online!
- Join a monthly drawing challenge, like Inktober[4], or the Sketchnote London group[5], where Dr Makayla Lewis[6] publishes a regular monthly sketchnote challenge
- Do a challenge with a friend; that way, it's more motivating, and you've got something extra to celebrate together at the end

The more places you try out your sketching powers, the more uses you'll find for sketching!

---

4. http://www.inktober.com/

5. https://www.meetup.com/sketchnoteLDN/

6. https://twitter.com/maccymacx

GET INTO A
SKETCHBOOK
HABIT

TRY MAKING YOUR MEETINGS AT WORK
MORE VISUAL WITH THE WHITEBOARD

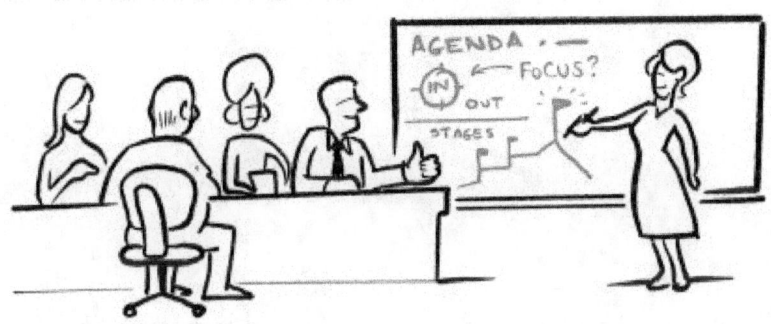

SHARE YOUR
SKETCHES ON
SOCIAL MEDIA

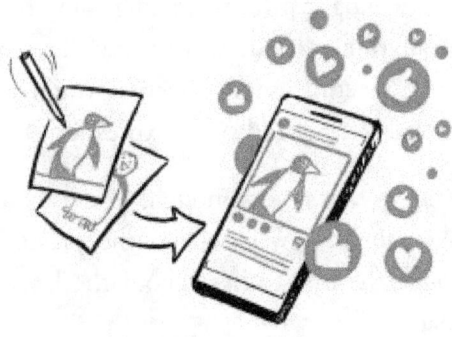

Get more sketching tips and tricks

If you like this kind of sketching, and you want to dig into more examples and exercises, check out my other book, called *Presto Sketching*[7], which goes into lots of different aspects about sketching to think better and communicate better.

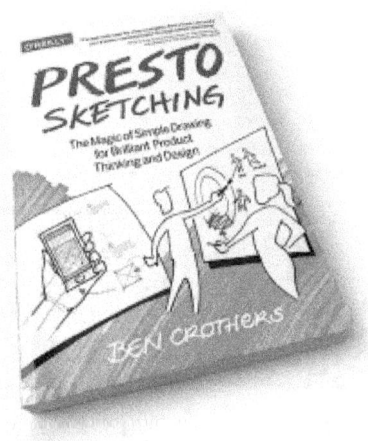

Be sure to take a look at the various tips and techniques that I share on the blog at prestosketching.com[8], too. From adding more creativity to anything you draw, to using different patterns on whiteboards to make meetings more effective, you're sure to find ways of improving your sketching and visual expression there.

And if that's not enough, you can always sign up to the Presto Sketching e-newsletter, on the Presto Sketching website. That way, you're the first to hear about the latest tips and news that I have to share.

---

7. *http://prestosketching.com/*

8. http://prestosketching.com/

Follow Presto Sketching on social media

Take a look at the @prestosketching[9] handle on Instagram; I'm probably still adding new four-step practice sketches as you read this! I also share other things to do with visual thinking and communication on Facebook[10] and Twitter[11].

I'm always open to suggestions too, so if there's a particular thing that you'd like to see broken down as four steps, just let me know by emailing me at prestosketching@gmail.com, and I'll do my best to add it to the feed.

Happy sketching!

---

9. http://instagram.com/prestosketching

10. https://www.facebook.com/prestosketching/

11. http://twitter.com/prestosketching

Don't miss out!

Visit the website below and you can sign up to receive emails whenever Ben Crothers publishes a new book. There's no charge and no obligation.

https://books2read.com/r/B-A-GBLH-UPRW

BOOKS 2 READ

Connecting independent readers to independent writers.

About the Author

Ben Crothers is on a mission to help as many people as possible think better and solve problems better by drawing better. We're inundated with so much information every day, and visual thinking is becoming more and more crucial to making sense of it all. Simple drawing is a fantastic shortcut to thinking better, and expressing ourselves better.

Ben has been a designer and facilitator for over 20 years, and a teacher of visual communication and facilitation for a good chunk of that time, too. His first book, *Presto Sketching: The Magic of Simple Drawing for Brilliant Product Thinking and Design* (O'Reilly) has helped loads of people all over the world to increase their visual thinking and sketching confidence.

Ben lives with his wife and two children in Sydney, Australia. When not drawing, designing or teaching, he's often found at the beach or at the barbecue... or both!

Read more at drawin4.com.

www.ingramcontent.com/pod-product-compliance
Lightning Source LLC
Chambersburg PA
CBHW051535170526
45165CB00002B/735